Bohemians: A Very Short Introduction

T0016643

VERY SHORT INTRODUCTIONS are for anyone wanting a stimulating and accessible way into a new subject. They are written by experts, and have been translated into more than 45 different languages.

The series began in 1995, and now covers a wide variety of topics in every discipline. The VSI library currently contains over 700 volumes—a Very Short Introduction to everything from Psychology and Philosophy of Science to American History and Relativity—and continues to grow in every subject area.

Very Short Introductions available now:

For more information visit our website

www.oup.com/vsi/

David Weir

BOHEMIANS

A Very Short Introduction

OXFORD
UNIVERSITY PRESS

Oxford University Press is a department of the University of Oxford.
It furthers the University's objective of excellence in research, scholarship,
and education by publishing worldwide. Oxford is a registered trade mark of
Oxford University Press in the UK and in certain other countries.

Published in the United States of America by Oxford University Press
198 Madison Avenue, New York, NY 10016, United States of America.

CIP data is on file at the Library of Congress

ISBN 978-0-19-753829-6

Printed and bound by
CPI Group (UK) Ltd, Croydon, CR0 4YY

*In memory of Kyle Andrew Weir and
David Geoffrey Weir*

Contents

List of illustrations

Acknowledgments

If I were a bohemian (and I might well be), these are the people I would want to spend time with in a leaky loft or a seedy bar: Bénédicte Coste of the Université de Bourgogne; Esther Bell, Kathy Morris, and David Murphy of the Sterling and Francine Clark Art Institute; Lucy Sante of Bard College; Jane Desmarais of Goldsmiths, University of London; Katharina Herold-Zanker of Durham University; Gabriel Emmett Quigley of New York University; Melanie Hawthorne of Texas A&M University; Rachel Ruisard of Oxford University Press; and, of course, Nancy Toff, the infallible editor of this Very Short Introduction who merits not only very special thanks, but also a very special bottle of Bordeaux. Finally, I thank *ma femme bohème*, Camille, for all the support she has given me over the course of my vagabond career.

Introduction

Bohemians are urban gypsies, or gypsy-artists, moving about from one derelict neighborhood to another, nourished only by their dreams and their hatred of bourgeois society, living wherever they can—a garret, a basement, an unheated studio—provided the rent is cheap and the morals are loose. That, at least, is the prevailing myth, which started in the nineteenth century when Romantic writers such as George Sand (Amantine Lucile Aurore Dupin) compared poets and artists to vagabonds from Bohemia, the supposed home of the Romany people once known by the racist term *gypsy* (who did not originate in Egypt, as the name "gypsy" suggests, but India). The thing about this myth, however, is that it seems to be largely true, or, at least, partly true, since the poets and artists who were compared to ethnic Bohemians really did cultivate the "bohemian" life, even before Sand and others named it as such.

Here it would be useful to think about what *myth* means: Aristotle and other Greek thinkers used the word μῦθος (transliterated as *mȳthos*) to mean "plot" or "story," which is why the *Oxford English Dictionary* defines the word as "[a] traditional story, typically involving supernatural beings or forces, which embodies and provides an explanation . . . or justification for something such as the early history of a society, a religious belief or ritual, or a natural phenomenon." The myth of Bohemia does not involve any supernatural beings, but it does involve some "supercultural" ones in addition to Sand, such as Henry Murger, who was something of a hack journalist before he published a series of feuilletons, or newspaper sketches, about the impoverished lives he and his artist friends led in Paris during the 1840s. These semi-fictional stories later provided the basis for a highly successful play, which in turn served as the main source for the version of the myth that almost everyone knows: Giacomo Puccini's opera *La Bohème* (1896).

So the myth, or story, of Bohemia started out as a way of explaining not a natural phenomenon, as most myths do, but a cultural phenomenon: the transformation of the meaning of art and the nature of artists as the era of modernity unfolded. That era involved the reconfiguration of social classes (the rise of the bourgeoisie); the realignment of political power (the growth of republican governance); and the transition to new economic models (the development of capitalism). This is a lot for one myth to handle, so it is not surprising that along the way the story outstripped the history it was originally supposed to explain. Does that mean that today the story is more familiar than the history? Not exactly. Given that both the history and the myth of Bohemia originate in Paris, we would do well to remember that in French *history* and *story* are the same word: *histoire*.

This linguistic factoid is quite useful because it suggests a larger truth about the cultural phenomenon we are trying to understand: namely, that bohemian culture seems to occupy some kind of shifting middle ground *between* myth and history. Moreover, that intermediate or mediating condition appears to do a lot of work in other areas as well, especially the political, because the bohemian myth begins just as Western society starts to feel the parallel economic and ideological effects of the dual Industrial and French Revolutions that allowed the new commercial class known as the bourgeoisie to flourish. The fictional bohemians Murger described in his newspaper stories, in his play, and finally in his book titled

Scènes de la vie de bohème (*Scenes of Bohemian Life*, 1851, but often "translated" *Bohemians of the Latin Quarter*) may have appeared in the middle of the nineteenth century, but the real ones who prompted him to call his characters *bohémiens* had been around at least since the 1830s, when the French Romantic movement gained impetus from its antagonism to the wealthy bourgeoisie, supporters of Louis Philippe. Not for nothing is his reign (1830–48) known to this day as "the bourgeois monarchy," one ramification of which was the continuing attenuation of royal support for the arts that put artists at the mercy of the market, an economic development which had begun even before Louis Philippe assumed the throne.

From the first, then, bohemians and bourgeoisie contested one another on the grounds of class and culture, the bohemians driven by the desire for personal liberty and the bourgeoisie by the need for economic security. This much is clear, despite the difficulty of saying precisely what the categories "bohemian" and "bourgeoisie" really mean. At first, "bohemian" seems to be more of a cultural sensibility than an economic class, the reverse of bourgeoisie, which is more clearly defined as a class than a culture. The political philosopher Raymond Williams says that "bourgeois" was originally "a juridical category in society, defined by such conditions as length of residence. The essential definition was that of the solid citizen whose mode of life was at once stable and solvent." By contrast, bohemians usually have no interest in being "solid citizens" and often take perverse pride in impoverishment, an economic condition that is also a signifier of class. And there is a type of culture more closely identified with the bourgeoisie than with bohemians, namely, commercial culture, which is traditional, not avant-garde.

The term *avant-garde*, originally a military term referring to the forward-most troops doing reconnaissance work for the main army to follow, implies that artists who are in the cultural avant-garde will ultimately find their work appreciated by the rest

3

of society whose aesthetic tastes will one day catch up to them. So, if the bohemian avant-garde, however far in advance of the traditional culture of the bourgeoisie it might be, will ultimately be appreciated by the bourgeoisie, that means they must have something in common. Perhaps bohemians belong to a culture first and a class second, and the bourgeoisie to class first and culture second. But however the relationship between the two is understood, the categories "bohemian" and "bourgeoisie" condition one another in various ways. Is "bohemian" the name for the low social stage through which avant-garde culture passes on the way to bourgeois respectability? Perhaps, but the inverse of that dynamic also occurs, when the respectable, cultured bourgeoisie seeks acceptance into the low social world of the bohemian. In other words, the mutual antagonism of bohemians and bourgeoisie is not absolute; rather, "bohemianism" appears to mediate the extremes, its shifting middle ground allowing for the intersection of political sensibilities that, in other contexts, are usually separate.

The scare quotes around "bohemianism" are meant as a caution against the assumption that there is anything unified or systematic about what bohemians do or how they live, which is what an -*ism* suffix usually implies. The French poet Charles Baudelaire, an important bohemian in his own right (at least for a while), may have been the first to use the term *bohemianism* when he gave this advice to himself in one of his journals: "To glorify vagabondage and what may be called bohemianism [*le Bohémianisme*]," adding, "cult of the multiple sensations expressed by music. Refer here to Liszt." The Hungarian composer Franz Liszt collected folk tunes from the region of Bohemia, in what was then the Austrian Empire, and used them in 1847 to compose the Hungarian Rhapsody no. 2, also known as the Bohemian Rhapsody (not to be confused with the rock anthem by the British band Queen). The Liszt reference, however, may be less important than Baudelaire's association of *Bohémianisme* with glorifying vagabondage and experiencing "multiple sensations," which in the case of Baudelaire and other bohemians came about not only by means of music but also drugs, especially hashish. As Baudelaire discovered, a hashish high allowed him to experience the vagabond life without ever leaving his room, a mode of travel favored by innumerable bohemians since.

The bohemian myth is so much a part of French cultural history (which in turn has influenced all other manifestations of bohemian culture) that it makes sense to pause over Baudelaire's coinage of *Bohémianisme* and consider additional French words associated with the phenomenon: *Bohême*, *bohème*, and *bohémien*. *Bohême*, with the circumflex accent over the first *e* (indicating that an *s* was dropped from *Boesme*, an earlier form of the word), is a place name that originally referred to a region, formerly a kingdom, that is now part of the modern Czech Republic. An inhabitant of *Bohême*—whether real or imaginary—was first *un bohême*, then *un bohème*, with a grave accent (the English translation for the title of Puccini's opera *La Bohème*, then, would be *The Bohemian*), but *bohème* is also an adjective, later written *bohèmien*. That form of the adjective does double duty as a noun—or did, until dictionary makers corrected it to *bohémien*, with an acute accent, since the rules of French pronunciation generally place the emphasis on the last syllable. The feminine form of both the adjective and the noun is *bohémienne*, the relative rarity of that word indicating the sociological fact that, at least until the late nineteenth century, almost all bohemians were men. In English, capitalized *Bohemia* can refer either to the geographical place or the imaginary place (depending on context), and *bohemians*—ungendered in English—refers to men and women who populate the imaginary cultural country called Bohemia.

Bohemia, then, is a metaphor that compares artists to vagabonds, people who have no stable place of residence. That metaphor can be extended to include a key fact about the changing social conditions of art itself, with the artist becoming a kind of "gypsy" moving from one patron or audience to another. Prior to the post-revolutionary era when the idea of the bohemian emerged, a musician, say, who enjoyed the patronage of a prince or other aristocrat also enjoyed a measure of social stability. When art became unmoored from the patron system, the artist was free to move around, to go from place to place, to seek an audience wherever commercial realities allowed. That market model likening the artist's vagabond career to the "gypsy" life helps to explain part of the bohemian myth, but not all of it, for two reasons. First, bohemians seem uninterested in "commercial realities" and are not so itinerant after all: yes, they move around but with certain exceptions (the Beat Generation "on the road") that movement is largely confined to down-market urban neighborhoods like the Latin Quarter of nineteenth-century Paris on the Left Bank (south of the river Seine), so called because Latin had been the language of instruction at the Sorbonne, the college of the University of Paris located in the area that was dedicated to the study of theology during the Middle Ages. Second, not all bohemians are artists.

The French sociologist Pierre Bourdieu makes the important observation that the theory of "art for art's sake," which the first bohemians adopted in 1830s Paris, "breaks with the bourgeois lifestyle" because it rejects "all social justification of art and the artist." Bohemians have no obligations to the larger society, Bourdieu says, because they cultivate "the art of living" by fostering "a genuine society within society." For those original bohemians of the 1830s and for many of their successors, it was just as important to "live art" as to make art. But if art is something you live rather than something you make, that also means you do not have to be an artist to live like one, even if only on the weekends. For this reason, the fictional myth of Bohemia may be as important as the actual history of Bohemia, which is another way of saying that myth and history are interconnected and entangled.

The first bohemians that Bourdieu describes who lived in the Latin Quarter and other parts of Paris in the 1830s may not have been the first in fact—the eighteenth-century artists, actors, writers, and engravers who lived and drank in the pubs and coffee houses of "the Town" (an area around Covent Garden in London) might antedate them, but the Paris group was almost certainly the first in name. *Les Bohémiens*, a novel published in 1790 by the obscure libertine author Anne Gédéon Lafitte, marquis de Pelleport, does describe a vagabond band of exiled writers as "bohemians," but the book failed so completely that it had no influence on later authors. The journalist Félix Pyat makes no mention of Pelleport in 1834, the date that marks the first use of the term *Bohémien* in its modern, familiar sense. In "Les Artistes," an essay that appeared in a collection by various authors describing aspects of "Paris Moderne," Pyat identifies artists not so much as members of a profession or practitioners of a craft but as devotees of a holy order: "[A]rt itself is a belief and the true artist is a priest of this eternal religion which differs from all others because it creates rather than destroys."

Pyat is at pains to nail down the nature of "the true artist" because, he claims, the identity has lately been assumed by just about everyone, including "[h]airdressers, vaudeville performers, glaziers, theater impresarios, pedicurists, café waiters, politicians, [and] shoe polishers," along with "learned dogs" and "trained elephants." This *"artistisme"* (artistism) is the disease of the age, "a scourge worse than cholera" that is quickly spreading everywhere. True art is a calling, not a job like hairdressing or waiting tables, and those who answer that calling are "today's Bohemians." When Pyat used the term, he was counting on his reader to know what a bohemian was—a nomad with no firm connections to the larger society (the vagabond life of the "gypsy" apparently lies behind Pyat's stress on the importance of "flâneuring," a flâneur being one who wanders around observing the life of the city).

"Bohemians" explained—for the first time

God created all this and, if we believe Genesis, he created it in six days. He spent the entire seventh day flâneuring, artist that he is. He continues to flâneur to this day, and he made the artist in his image.

But if God is an artist, the artist is also God since art is life, energy, creation. God is the patron saint of artists, just as St. Eligius is for goldsmiths or St. George for soldiers....And how qualified one must be to march under such a banner! The bar is set high for those who join such a movement. The title of "artist" isn't reserved strictly for poets, painters, sculptors, musicians, architects, actors, or dancers; it belongs to all those whose spirits have been creative....

The obsession common among young artists of wanting to live outside their own time, with other ideas and other customs, cuts them off from the world, turns them into outsiders and eccentrics, places them beyond the law and banishes them from society. These are today's Bohemians.

Thus, they have a language of their own: the slang of the artists' studio, unintelligible to the rest of humanity....

They use the term *bourgeois* for anyone who isn't one of them, just as the Romans used to refer to barbarians....

They're at that age when one doesn't understand life's material comforts...; furthermore, even though they lack grand political convictions, artists nonetheless hate more than anyone those who prostitute their beliefs, who change allegiances as the wind blows, who become slaves to money, material goods, and coarse pleasures.

—Felix Payat, "Les Artistes" (1834)

Despite Pyat's differentiation of "artistism" from true art, with the bohemian emerging as a more genuine artist than a hairdresser, his discussion of "the Bohemians of today" is still laced with considerable irony. But Pyat's role in the story of Bohemia is not limited to his 1834 essay. In 1831, Pyat helped George Sand start her literary career when he introduced her to the editor of *Le Figaro*, the Paris newspaper founded in 1826. In her autobiography, Sand describes Pyat as one of three literary apprentices on the staff of the paper who came from the old province of Berry (where she had been raised by her grandmother), the other two being herself and Jules Sandeau. Sand and Sandeau had a brief love affair, but, more important for her career, they also collaborated on a novel, *Rose et blanche, ou la comédienne et la religieuse* (Pink and white, or the actress and the nun), published in 1831 under the pseudonym Jules Sand—the partial origin of her pen name, while "George," she thought, "seemed to me appropriate for someone from rural Berry." Back in Paris, where she was born, Sand the journalist adopted a male mode of dress, which allowed her to move about the city more freely.

As she says in her autobiography, "My clothing made me fearless." She also smoked like a man, and since tobacco is supposed to be what bohemians value most in the world (according to Pyat), Sand must be regarded as a bohemian *avant la lettre*, at least in the early 1830s. In any event, it was she more than any other author of the period who established "the vagabond vocation of the bohemian artist," as she put it in a novel of 1842, as a positive ideal. But it was in an earlier novel, *La dernière Aldine* (*The Last Aldini*, 1837), that Sand explored the meaning of the bohemian artist in full and included most of the elements that will come to comprise the broader myth of Bohemia in the years to come: the disdain for material wealth and comfort, the superiority of artists to their presumed social betters, the love of liberty, and so on, all of which is encompassed by the main character's removal from "the customs of the world, and the laws of society."

1. The young George Sand dressed as a "newspaperman" at the outset of her career so she could go places in Paris where women were not supposed to go.

That sentiment squares with Pyat's notion of the artist as someone who lives outside the law. Such thinking is highly suggestive of the ideology of anarchism, which Pyat himself was to embrace much later in life, when he became a member of the Paris Commune, the short-lived anarcho-socialist society established on March 18, 1871, when the municipality of Paris (*la commune de Paris*) seceded from the nation of France (it lasted just over two months, until May 28). The less-than-liberal bohemians of the 1830s notwithstanding, later adherents of the kind of anti-bourgeoise calling Pyat described often gravitated toward anarchism, and here the story becomes somewhat contradictory. Bohemians are always avant-garde or forward-looking in art and literature, but, like their Romantic precursors, they have certain preferences for the past and remain proudly out of step with the march of progress. They like their modernity handmade, not industrially produced. In this respect they have much in common with the nineteenth-century anarchists who were contemporary with bohemians and sometimes identical with them, as was the case with the painter Gustave Courbet, friend of Joseph Proudhon (one of the founders of anarchism) and a participant, like Pyat, in the Paris Commune.

The bohemian-anarchist concord in the case of the Commune goes a long way toward explaining the peculiar relationship bohemians have with the cities they love—they are *in* them but not *of* them. That is, they do not live in cites so much as neighborhoods, and the more run-down and removed those neighborhoods are from more upscale bourgeois sectors the better. In some cases, the neighborhood where bohemians live might not have been a part of the surrounding city for very long: such was the case with Montmartre, which was not incorporated into the city of Paris until 1859 and maintained the feel of a separate village well into the twentieth century.

Montmartre attracted artists like Henri de Toulouse-Lautrec in the nineteenth century and Pablo Picasso in the early twentieth not only because of the low cost of living, but also because the laws and regulations (covering the sale of alcohol, for instance) that obtained in greater Paris did not fully apply to the village-in-the-city. A version of this pattern is repeated in other cities: even when the laws and regulations governing a particular section of the metropolis were on the books, they were not always strictly enforced in those areas where bohemians congregated. The kind of freedom that painters enjoyed in Montmartre, poets also enjoyed in the Schwabing borough of Munich, socialists in the Greenwich Village neighborhood of New York City, surrealists in the Montparnasse quarter of Paris, and so on. This component of bohemian life—the alignment of land and liberty, whereby the neighborhood becomes a kind of autonomous "nation" unto itself and the usual norms and laws do not apply—is both real and imaginary. Or rather, the reality is infused with the imaginary and subordinated to it, such that *where* the bohemian lives is not so much the aforementioned Montmartre, Schwabing, Greenwich Village, or Montparnasse, but Bohemia itself.

Chapter 1
Fictional Bohemias

On March 20, 1893, the Italian composer and librettist Ruggiero Leoncavallo published a notice in the Milan newspaper *Il Secolo* announcing that he had been working on a new opera for some time, based on Henry Murger's *Scenes of Bohemian Life*. Leoncavallo says that anyone who doubts this claim can ask Victor Maurel, the baritone for whom the composer was writing the part of Schaunard, or the soprano Elisa Frandin, who "is able to testify that four months ago the Maestro spoke to her of the role of Musette." He mentions a recent meeting with his fellow composer Giacomo Puccini, who, according to Leoncavallo, came up with the idea of putting *La Bohème* to music just "a few days ago." Hence, "Maestro Leoncavallo's priority as regards this opera is indisputable." The next day, Puccini published a response in the newspaper *Il Corriere*, claiming ignorance of Leoncavallo's project, adding that had he known his friend was working on the new opera he "would not have thought of Murger's *Bohème*." Puccini says he has been working on the opera for two months, but, unlike Leoncavallo, he offers no witnesses to support the claim. But what does it matter? "Let him compose and I will compose," Puccini says, "and the public will judge. Precedence in art does not imply that one must interpret the same subject with the same artistic ideas."

Puccini was right: the public has since judged his operatic treatment of Murger's bohemians as preferable to the one by Leoncavallo, which is rarely performed, whereas Puccini's is part of the repertory of every opera house in the world. Puccini was likewise correct in stating that the same subject can be interpreted in a variety of ways. Indeed, his own version of the story of the poet Rodolfo, the painter Marcello, the composer Schaunard, and the philosopher Colline, along with the grisette Mimì and the demimondaine Musetta (to give the Italian names of the characters) departs in many ways from the French original. Originals plural would be more accurate, since the basis for the opera is not only Murger's newspaper feuilletons but also the play based on those pieces, not to mention the book Murger published after the success of the play. Puccini's opera is a kind of composite of the book and the play, even though he leaves out elements of both, such as the character Phémie, Schaunard's lover, and Durandin, Rodolphe's uncle, a character added to the play by Murger's collaborator.

Puccini's *La Bohème*, then, is only one version of the story about the unconventional lives of starving artists that will be retold many times over in novels, plays, and films. However original the characters might have appeared to the audience for the opera when it premiered in Milan in 1896, today it is hard to see them as anything other than stereotypes, clichéd versions of arty French culture. Hence, there is a kind of poetic justice in the fact that the idea of Bohemia that Puccini popularized in the form of Italian opera singers impersonating stereotypical French artists was first given narrative form by a French author who construed bohemians as clichéd versions of Italian opera singers.

George Sand's *The Last Aldini* (1838) is the first extended exploration of bohemian life in the form of a novel. The story is told from the point of view of a famous Italian opera singer called Lélio, who started out life as the son of a fisherman from Chioggia, a small city on the coast of the Adriatic Sea south of Venice.

Lélio recounts how he left the fishing village for Venice to work as a gondolier at the Aldini Palace. There, he astonishes the aristocrats with the power of his voice, even though he has had no formal musical training. Impressed, the Countess Bianca Aldini supports and encourages his singing. One night, the gondola is stranded on the marsh when the tide goes out and the countess confesses her secret love for Lélio. They have their "nuptial night" on the gondola, but it turns out to be their "only night of love, a pure night which never recurred." Lélio leaves the countess for reasons of class: he cannot betray his humble origins by marrying above his station. He is also concerned that if Signora Aldini marries below her class, the Aldini family will take her daughter away from her (she married young, and her husband was killed in a duel). So Lélio returns to his father in Chioggia.

Ten years pass, and Lélio, now in Florence, has established himself as a successful tenor. One of his friends is a soprano known as "the Checchina," also from Chioggia with a fisherman father, but the reader who thinks this well-matched pair will end up a couple would be wrong. The Checchina is not the marrying type, preferring the wandering life of an opera singer. In fact, she breaks off an affair with a nobleman named Nasi when he proposes marriage. As for Lélio, he falls in love with another young aristocrat who catches his eye at one of his performances. He wants to marry her but is concerned that the Romantic democracy of his ideas might be an impediment to the union. She assures him that her widowed mother will approve the marriage, but when Lélio meets the mother he discovers that she is none other than Bianca Aldini. Her daughter, Alezia, "the last of the Aldini," promptly faints, but when she comes to her senses she consents to marry that same Nasi the Checchina spurned. In the end, Lélio is free to resume the wandering life of the singing bohemian.

The class consciousness that informs Sand's early exploration of bohemian life in *The Last Aldini* also finds its way into one of Honoré Balzac's short novels, *The Prince of Bohemia*, first

Bohemian superiority to society

An artist...has the whole world for his country, *la grande Bohême*, as we say.

...We *Bohémians* are not much moved by the customs of the world, and the laws of society; we have no great fear of defeat on those private stages, where the world in its turn, bows before us, and where we completely feel the superiority of the artist; for there, no one can excite in us the lively emotions which we know so well how to arouse. The *salons* fatigue and chill us, in return for the warmth and life we carry into them....[L]et us leave them to weary themselves without us. Let us despise the pride of the great, laugh at their follies, spend our wealth gaily when we have it and endure poverty without complaint should it come. Above all let us preserve our liberty, enjoy life, and *vive la Bohême.*

—George Sand, *The Last Aldini* (1838)

published in a magazine in 1840 and later incorporated into the author's vast panorama of modern life known as *The Human Comedy*. The novella was written slightly before Balzac had the idea of linking the narratives set during the Bourbon Restoration (1815–30) and the July Monarchy (1830–48) through recurring characters and other devices, but it can be read as part of his social commentary during the latter of the two political eras *The Human Comedy* involves. Balzac's description of Bohemia seems rather limited because of the focus on only one bohemian character, the fantastically named Gabriel Jean Anne Victor Benjamin George Ferdinand Charles Edward Rusticoli, Comte de la Palférine, more simply known as La Palférine. Given the political history of France, his aristocratic pedigree is no guarantee of wealth, so he is left "to live by his easel." His aristocratic background accounts for the social ease La Palférine exhibits both in his strained economic conditions and in his entitled relationships with women.

One day he sees an attractive woman and begins to escort her along the street and into a shop as if he were her husband. The elegant dress of the woman suggests that she might be nobility, but on reflection La Palférine concludes that after July 1830 she can only be "a princess of the stage." Sure enough, the woman is—or was—a dancer called Claudine, married to a playwright named Bruel. The affair proceeds well enough until La Palférine tires of her, whereupon he makes what he thinks is an impossible demand: that Claudine acquire sufficient trappings of wealth to dupe society and pass for real royalty: "[O]ne day La Palférine said, 'If you wish to be the mistress of one La Palférine, poor, penniless, and without prospects as he is, you ought at least to represent him worthily. You should have a carriage and liveried servants and a title." Astonishingly, after a few years Claudine satisfies her lover's demand by manipulating her husband to outfit her in aristocratic finery, contriving to acquire a coat of arms, and styling herself "La Comtesse du Bruel." La Palférine is both surprised and moved by this development, but not enough to resume the affair. Instead, with tears in his eyes, he tells her, "I will do something for you; I will put you—in my will."

Aside from the reference to the arrogant La Palférine "living by his easel" and his uncertain finances, there is little about Balzac's novel to suggest what the character's bohemian life consists of at an everyday level. Instead, the author provides descriptions of the Bohemia La Palférine is supposed to inhabit, many of them sufficiently detailed to suggest that by 1840 the idea of Bohemia had already begun to acquire the status of convention, if not quite cliché.

> Bohemianism, which by rights should be called the doctrine of the
> Boulevard des Italiens, finds its recruits among young men between
> twenty and thirty, all of them men of genius in their way, little

known, it is true, as yet, but sure of recognition one day, and when that day comes, of great distinction.... There are writers, administrators, soldiers, and artists in Bohemia; every faculty, every kind of brain is represented there. Bohemia is a microcosm. If the Czar would buy Bohemia for a score of millions and set its population down in Odessa—always supposing that they consented to leave the asphalt of the boulevards—Odessa would be Paris within the year.

At the same time, some parts of Balzac's description of Bohemia seem a bit off today. The Boulevard des Italiens, so named because of its proximity to the Theatre des Italiens, an opera house, had been paved in 1830 and was a fashionable place for prominent citizens to promenade and be seen. Perhaps there were some bohemians among the more well-off types strolling on the glamorous boulevard, but it was hardly a bohemian neighborhood. It may be that Balzac's notion of Bohemia was more expansive than it has since become, as his inclusion of administrators and soldiers among the more expected writers and artists suggests. Still, Balzac's identification of the bohemian sensibility as insistently Parisian is certainly right (for the time), as Murger affirmed a decade later in his preface to *Scenes of Bohemian Life*: "Bohemia only exists and is only possible in Paris."

Murger's bohemian narrative is undoubtedly more familiar in the operatic adaptation by Puccini, which emphasizes the tragic love affair between Rodolfo and Mimì (as does Leoncavallo's 1897 opera). But the popularity of Puccini is unfortunate for a couple of reasons. For one, the characters in Murger's telling all have a rather ambivalent relationship to the bohemian values they allegedly embody. In truth, they all have day jobs, so to speak, that betray a certain desire for social mobility, their aim being to secure for themselves a more reliable, secure existence that, if attained, would make them bourgeois, not bohemian. For example, Colline the "hyperphysical" philosopher finances the speculative life "by giving lessons in rhetoric, mathematics, and several other *ics*."

2. A caricature of the prematurely bald Henry Murger shows the writer constantly weeping because of a disease diagnosed at the time as "purpura."

Rodolphe writes poetry and drama, but he also has a steady if limited income as the editor of two magazines, *The Scarf of Iris* (a fashion journal) and *The Beaver* (dealing with the hat trade). Marcel works tirelessly on his masterpiece *The Parting of the Red Sea*, submitting versions of it year after year to the official salon in hope of gaining state recognition as an artist, but he also does portrait work for money. Schaunard may labor over his eccentric compositions, such as *Symphony on the Influence of Blue in Art*, but he is not above giving music lessons to keep himself and his friends in tobacco and wine. And not just any wine—they are partial to Côte de Beaune, a fine Burgundy.

The other element that is less pronounced in Puccini's opera is the humor of the book. There are many moments when the relations between the characters are couched in comic terms, as with the first meeting, at a restaurant, between Colline and Schaunard. They both order rabbit stew, but there is only one serving left, which goes to Colline, who has ordered first. Colline sees how disappointed Schaunard is and offers to share his stew with him but insists on eating the head. Schaunard discovers that his half of the stew also includes a head, whereupon Colline exclaims, "Good heavens!...It is a bicephalous rabbit!" He notes that the eighteenth-century French naturalist Buffon "cites some cases of this monstrosity" and seems genuinely to believe that he is eating "a phenomenon" without considering the more obvious explanation that the cook made the stew out of more than one rabbit.

The two-headed rabbit is an isolated joke, but there are any number of running gags with the bohemians' various long-suffering landlords. Rodolphe, for example, flatters one of them by saying, "It is extraordinary, Monsieur Benoît, but every time I think of your triple character as a landlord, a bootmaker, and a friend I am tempted to believe in the Trinity." Many clever turns of phrase dot the book. After Schaunard performs one of his compositions, "an exultant grimace...mounted over his nose like a circumflex accent." The English-speaking reader who knows what such an accent looks like (as in, say, Bohême) can appreciate the fanciful comparison, but the book also includes many puns that do not come across in English. One meaning of Benoît, the name of Rodolphe's landlord, is "blessed," an ironic epithet given his difficulties collecting rent from his bohemian tenants. At one point Rodolphe does hackwork writing a manual on stove cleaning for his uncle, whose motto is "Nascuntur poê…liers," which means "stove-makers are born," a joking variation on the Latin maxim drawn from Cicero, "Nascuntur poetae" (poets are born).

Finally, Murger's humor involves not only flashes of verbal wit and the occasional set-piece, but whole chapters, one of which is especially funny. Chapter 21 is titled "Romeo and Juliet" because Rodolphe, having recently broken up with Mimi for the second time, has taken to fashioning himself Romeo because his new mistress is named Juliet. Rodolphe has charmed this Juliet by "sonneteering" her with his tongue and hands in his apartment, but she will never stay over, always leaving at midnight, so he devises a plan to spend the night at her place. He is on his way to the woman's apartment when he runs into Colline on the street. The philosopher wonders why his friend is carrying a rope ladder and a pigeon in a cage, and Rodolphe explains that he plans to use the ladder to scale his Juliet's balcony. He adds that the bird is not a pigeon but a clock, which will serve instead of the nightingale in Shakespeare's play to awaken the couple in the morning after a night of lovemaking. In the play, Juliet says, "Wilt thou be gone? it is not yet near day. / It was the nightingale, and not the lark," and Romeo replies, "It was the lark, the herald of the morn."

After rehearsing the scene with Colline, Rodolphe goes to Juliet's apartment and finds that the "balcony" is on the ground floor, so he clambers over it with ease and makes love to Juliet all night long. Because they never go to sleep, the lovers are awake when the "nightingale" starts to sing—or coo—at 5:00 a.m. Since they are both famished from all the lovemaking, they decide to get up and have breakfast. All Juliet has are some onions, bacon, bread, and butter. So: "Romeo looked at Juliet, Juliet looked at Romeo, and both looked at the pigeon." The bird is still singing, but "it was the song of the swan": "Romeo and Juliet grilled their clock." The lovers comment on the bird's tender voice and flesh, gazing at one another with tears in their eyes, whereupon the narrator comments: "Hypocrites, it was the onions that made them weep."

The last line of "Romeo and Juliet" obviously satirizes sentimental romance, as does the whole story, with its realistic account of a love affair. Another stand-alone chapter, by contrast, takes romance seriously—despite occasional flashes of wit—and must be regarded as the single most important chapter to the myth of Bohemia as it developed in the years to come. "Francine's Muff" is one of the few stories in the collection written in the first-person, the narrative voice in this case being very close to Murger's own, if not identical with it: "Amongst the true Bohemians of the real Bohemia I used to know one named Jacques D.," a sculptor. Here Murger evokes one of the categories of bohemians identified in his preface, "those called by art" who "have the chance of being also amongst its elect."

The story begins with Jacques's funeral to set the stage for the sculptor's extreme poverty: he is so poor he is buried without a shroud. Murger then builds up the retrospective account of Jacques's life, including his love affair with Francine, who knocks on the door of his apartment because her candle has gone out, asking for a light. Jacques is on the point of obliging when a gust of wind blows out his own candle. When Francine drops her key on the floor of the darkened room, the two of them get on their hands and knees and search for it. Their hands touch, the moonlight fills the room, they talk. At length Francine sees the key on the floor, but without Jacques noticing it she pushes the key under some furniture.

Time passes, the lovers are happy, but Francine grows ill with tuberculosis. "She will go with the autumn leaves," a doctor tells Jacques. Francine overhears the dire prognosis but tells Jacques not to worry: "we will go and live in a pine forest, the leaves are always green there." As she is on her deathbed, Francine asks for a muff to keep her hands warm. After she dies, Jacques makes a plaster cast of her face, intending to make a funeral monument for her. At her funeral, as the coffin is lowered into the grave, Jacques cries out, "Oh! my youth, it is you they are burying." Rodolphe puts in a brief appearance when he counsels Jacques to console himself with a new mistress, explaining that he can continue to love the dead Francine: "You will embrace her on another's lips." Jacques's plans to memorialize Francine through his sculpture are cut short by his own illness—contracted from Francine—and the story concludes with the terse comment: "He is buried somewhere."

This summary does not adequately convey the deep sense of pathos in the story, its often-bitter realism saving it from the sentimentality that opera lovers relish as the story of Mimì and Rodolfo in Puccini's *La Bohème*. But Puccini was not the first to transform Francine into Mimì or to borrow elements from the character Jacques to embellish Rodolphe with the heart-breaking loss he feels when his lover dies. That distinction belongs to the dramatist Théodore Barrière, who had several vaudeville successes to his credit when he approached Murger with the idea of adapting the sketches of bohemian life that he had read in the newspaper into a play. Seeing his chance at fame—and income—at last, Murger happily agreed to the collaboration, not least because he had already contemplated the prospect of turning his newspaper work into a play. Barrière was a Murger fan, so he was not disappointed when he was introduced to the author of the newspaper sketches he so admired and found his idol living the bohemian life in reality. A mutual friend took Barrière to Murger's room on the top floor of a house (the higher the room, the lower the rent) during a rainstorm. Murger, who was still in bed at 3:00 p.m., advised his guest to keep his umbrella open because of the leaky roof and apologized for not getting out of bed—he had loaned his trousers to a friend who had yet to return them. Barrière was delighted: "But this is sheer Bohemia!" he exclaimed.

Murger accepted the offer of collaboration on the spot, and the two soon set about transforming the feuilletons into a play (presumably after Murger managed to reclaim his pants). Barrière may have been a bureaucrat (he worked at the Ministry of War), but he was also an experienced playwright with sound theatrical instincts. He should be credited with at least three modifications to the material at hand. First, he provided a plot by giving Rodolphe a rich uncle named Durandin, who pressures his nephew to marry a wealthy widow and become a respectable bourgeois gentleman. Second, he drew sharp lines of difference between Musette and Mimi, both of whom in their Murger versions are similarly unfaithful and often heartless but in the play those qualities are limited to Musette, while Mimi is made more sympathetic and sentimental. Third, and most important, Barrière adapted the stand-alone story "Francine's Muff" to the plot of the play, taking details from Jacques and Francine's meeting and transferring them to the story of Rodolphe and Mimi, as well as making Mimi die the heartbreaking death of Francine.

The first act of the play introduces Rodolphe at Durantin's estate in the provinces, resisting his uncle's plans for him to marry the wealthy widow Madame de Rouvre to guarantee a substantial income. Rodolphe insists on keeping his freedom, including the freedom "not to dine every day," a sentiment that aligns him with the bohemians he is shortly to meet. They are picnicking on the grounds of the estate when Rodolphe invites them all into the house and takes to them immediately—Marcel, Schaunard, Colline, Musette, and Phémie (who does not appear in the subsequent acts). Rodolphe expresses a wish to become a bohemian himself, and the party obliges by offering cover for his escape from his uncle's house, thereby avoiding the planned meeting with the wealthy widow.

The second act takes place a year later with Rodolphe leading the bohemian life in a cheap hotel room next to one occupied by his friend Marcel. The date is July 15th—Bastille Day—but also the day the rent comes due. Musette has left Marcel but Benoît, the landlord, rents Marcel's room to her when her former lover is out. Rodolphe is likewise evicted, and the room rented out to the poor orphan girl he fell in love with on a recent visit to the home for Abandoned Children. When the two friends return to find their rooms let to the women, Marcel grudgingly admits he still loves the faithless Musette and stays with her over Benoît's objections. Rodolphe, however, is more gallant and makes a show of morality before knocking on Mimi's door after Marcel and Musette refuse to let him into their room. The act ends with Mimi speechless at the prospect of spending the night with the man who asked to marry her at the orphanage.

Act III reveals Durantin to be the villain of the piece when he asks Mimi why she has not responded to his many letters explaining how much damage she is doing to Rodolphe's prospects by keeping him from marrying Madame de Rouvre. He tries to bribe her into leaving her lover and says he will disinherit Rodolphe if she does not. Mimi refuses the bribes but submits to the pressure and does as Durantin wishes; he tells his nephew that Mimi has been unfaithful to him, so Rodolphe reluctantly surrenders to his uncle's designs.

The fourth act is set at the home of Madame de Rouvre, who has staged a ball with the expectation that Rodolphe will propose to her. She makes the mistake of engaging Schaunard to play the piano at the ball, which means that his retinue of fellow bohemians also show up. Scandal ensues when Madame de Rouvre discovers Mimi, who flees in shame. When Rodolphe learns how his uncle has manipulated him and hears that Mimi has just left, he renounces both his uncle and Madame de Rouvre and leaves in pursuit of his beloved.

The final act finds Rodolphe, Marcel, Schaunard, and Colline in a cold room with the fire gone out and the wine bottles empty. Musette arrives, returning to Marcel yet again, telling him, "Each of my loves is a couplet, but you are the refrain"—and Marcel takes her back. Witnessing the reunion, Rodolphe is despondent: he has spent days looking for Mimi but cannot find her. At that moment, Mimi arrives, explaining that when she left Madame de Rouvre's she meant to throw herself into the Seine—"Just like a grisette in a novel"—but she faints on the bridge and wakes up in the Hôtel-Dieu; she has just come from the hospital. Rodolphe summons a doctor, who tells him, "My friend, she's finished." Mimi asks for a muff to keep her hands warm, whereupon Musette tells Marcel to go to her place and get one, which he does. In a surprising turn, Madame de Rouvre shows up, repentant over her treatment of Mimi, and offers to do anything to help. Durantin also appears, as insensitive as ever, but Musette puts him in his place: "I would like nothing more than to dissolve your fortune in the crucible of my caprices." Durantin, at last, softens: he takes both Rodolphe and Mimi by the hand and says, "I give him to you." Musette screams; Durantin releases Mimi's hand, which falls, lifeless. "Goodbye, Mimi," says Musette, while Rodolphe, overcome with grief, utters the curtain line lifted from the story, "Oh, my youth! It's you they're going to bury."

After the dress rehearsal for the play, Murger's friend the photographer Nadar found the curtain line "abominable," but Murger insisted it was "true to life." The opening-night audience must have agreed, because the play received immediate acclaim and had a successful run. Paris society seems to have turned out for the premiere on November 22, 1849, including Louis-Napoléon, the future emperor of France, then president prior to the coup he engineered in 1851. Marie-Christine Roux, the model for Musette, was also at the opening, not to mention those esteemed critics and former bohemians Théophile Gautier, Arsène Houssaye, and Théodore de Banville.

The synopsis gives the impression of a melodrama, and it is that—literally, because of the mixture of music and drama—but it is also a comedy, full of witty lines (as in Murger's stories). The staging of a play set in the 1840s after the failure of the 1848 revolution might well have been a factor in its success, since the post-revolutionary audience could look back on a segment of society that had played a role in the revolution with a knowing mixture of nostalgia and superiority. Indeed, the Murger-Barrière play probably represents the first time—but not the last—that a bourgeois audience would look upon bohemians as a source of public entertainment. That dynamic fairly describes the situation in Turin on February 1, 1896, when Puccini's *La Bohème* had its premiere at Teatro Regio.

Puccini's librettists Luigi Illica and Giuseppe Giacosa set the opera in 1830, the year when the bourgeois monarch Louis Philippe ascended to the throne. Back-dating Murger's narrative to the 1830s, the era of the original bohemians, heightens the comic contrast of the bourgeois-bohemian opposition, as when, in act I, Rodolfo sings, "Louis Philippe! I bow to my King!" (Luigi Filippo! / M'inchino al mio Re!). In fact, the poet is bowing to the image of the king on the coins the resourceful Schaunard secures by giving music lessons to an Englishman. The man has an annoying parrot he hates and tells Schaunard to play the piano until the bird dies, an ordeal Schaunard cuts short by poisoning the parrot with parsley. This bit of comic business is lifted from the book, but the most significant borrowing in the opera is taken from the play, namely Barrière's fusion of the characters Francine and Mimì, including the action at the end of Act I: Mimì comes to Rodolfo's room because her candle has gone out, then loses the key to her room. But the Mimì of the opera is not so clearly delineated from Musette as she is in the play; both are coquettish and inconstant.

3. The poster for the 1896 premiere of Puccini's *La Bohème* includes the name Henry Murger (on the banner above the word *Bohème*), but the credit is displayed far less prominently than the names of the librettists and the composer.

The Murger-Barrière Mimi is completely faithful to Rodolphe, while Puccini's Mimì leaves the poet for a viscount. All we know from the opera is that, according to Marcello, "She was in a carriage, / dressed like a queen" (Era in carrozza / vestita come una regina), and, later, according to Musetta, that Mimì has left the viscount. Critics sometimes describe these developments outside the stage action of Puccini's *La Bohème* as the opera's "missing act," which in Leoncavallo's competing version is presented in full. In act II of Leoncavallo's *La Bohème*, Musetta breaks things off with her rich patron, even as Mimì leaves Rodolfo for the viscount. In any event, in both versions Mimì returns to Rodolfo in the bohemians' garret at the end of the last act, affirming her love for the poet though fatally ill. Puccini's Mimì asks for a muff to warm her hands, as in the play, and dies, but here the librettists eschew the curtain line Murger defended against Nadar's critique, settling on Rodolfo's anguished—and minimalist—cry of "Mimì! Mimì!"

Despite initial tepid reviews and less-than-enthusiastic audience reception, *La Bohème* eventually became established as indispensable to the repertory of opera companies the world over. Two interrelated impediments to its success early on were the political environment of the still-young nation of Italy and the cultural context of operatic tradition. In the 1890s, French operas and operettas dominated the Italian stage, even as Italy's colonial enterprises had begun to founder. *La Bohème* premiered only weeks before Italian forces at Adwa in Abyssinia (present-day Ethiopia) suffered a humiliating defeat, so an Italian opera about French bohemians hardly met the need for cultural triumph in the face of national embarrassment. Possibly, the same social dynamic that obtained in the middle of the nineteenth century came to bear at the end, with bourgeois audiences finding popular entertainment value in an opera about down-and-out bohemians that offered a mixture of feel-good and feel-bad diversions from those same cultural and nationalistic currents that caused the critics to dismiss the work as insufficiently serious.

Early doubts about the artistic merits of Puccini's *La Bohème* may have been complicated by politics and culture, but once the opera caught on another reason emerged for dismissing its aesthetic worth: anything that popular could not possibly be good art. Paradoxically, this alleged lack of artistic merit appears to be one reason the opera has been so successful: the parts can be sung by journeyman performers and still be effective. Singers did not guarantee the success of the opera so much as the opera assured the success of the singers. At the same time, popular success attracted major singers to key roles, early examples being the celebrated Australian soprano Nellie Melba as Mimì and the great Italian tenor Enrico Caruso as Rodolfo (the two stars often appeared together). In short, the role that Puccini's opera has played in establishing the popular stereotype of bohemians as struggling artists who lead a life of pleasure in the face of restrictive bourgeois norms cannot be overstated.

The English conductor Thomas Beecham said that Puccini possessed "a highly developed inner visual sense" that gave him the ability to think theatrically and match his music to the drama. Beecham's insight about Puccini's visual imagination is borne out by the many film adaptations of *La Bohème*, which began— somewhat surprisingly—in the silent era of motion pictures. There were at least three silent shorts based on *La Bohème* in 1910–11, another in 1916, and a feature from 1926 directed by King Vidor, starring Lilian Gish as Mimi and John Gilbert as Rodolphe. The *New York Times* review of this film praises the portrayals of Mimi, Rodolphe, Musette, and "the impeccable Vicomte Paul" (who has no on-stage role in the Puccini opera). The *Times* critic also mentions "the special musical score" composed "to replace the Puccini music, which could not be played with the picture because of the copyright."

All told, the Internet Movie Database (IMDb) lists around sixty film versions of *La Bohème*, and while some of these are simply filmed performances rather than cinematic adaptations, the IMDb total is still an impressive number (for comparison, IMDb lists only eight film versions of Giuseppe Verdi's *La Traviata,* almost all filmed performances at major opera houses). The total does not include the many films that feature Puccini's music on the soundtrack, such as the hit romantic comedy *Moonstruck* (1987), where *La Bohème* is given kitsch treatment as part of the sentimental plot as well.

Of the many true adaptations, one stands out as representative of just how far removed from Murger's original narrative of bohemian life in 1840s France more recent imaginings have become: the hyperkinetic movie musical *Rent* (2005), directed by Chris Columbus. Based on the play by Jonathan Larson that opened off-Broadway in February 1996 and then moved to Broadway two months later, the film transposes Puccini's bohemians from the Latin Quarter circa 1830 to the East Village neighborhood of New York known as Alphabet City (because the avenues are identified by letters, not numbers) in 1989. The film conveys a less-than-plausible Hollywood version of the garbage-strewn streets and graffitied storefronts of downtown NYC in the late 1980s, where latter-day bohemians struggle to create their independent films and write their indie songs.

Most of the Puccini characters have been renamed, with the philosopher Colline becoming the scholarly Tom Collins (like the cocktail), Rodolfo the song-writer Roger, and Musetta the performance artist Maureen, whose inconstancy is now bisexual—she leaves the filmmaker Mark (counterpart of the painter Marcel in Murger) for a lawyer named Tracie. The one character who retains her eponymic identity is Mimi, now an exotic dancer instead of a flower-maker. The memorable candle scene is replayed when Mimi, unable to pay her utility bill, comes to Roger's apartment singing, "Light My Candle." Instead of her keys, she drops her drug stash on the floor, and as she crawls around with Roger looking on, she sings, "They say I have the best ass / below 14th Street. Is it true?" Instead of suffering from tuberculosis, this Mimi is HIV-positive, which makes Roger reluctant to submit to seduction, since his former lover died of AIDS.

Among the many tunes that stopped the show in its two theatrical incarnations is "La Vie Bohème," which includes such lyrics as: "The opposite of war isn't peace ... / It's creation," while Benny, the landlord villain of the piece (replacing the affable, bumbling Benoît of book, play, and opera), counters, "Bohemia, Bohemia's a fallacy in your head. / This is Calcutta / Bohemia is dead." Not so, sing the bohemians, "Woooooooo! / La vie Bohème ... / Viva la vie Bohème!" Complications ensue: the transsexual lover of one of the bohemians dies of AIDS, and Mimi, after almost shaking her heroin addiction, relapses and disappears. Her friends find her unconscious on the street and bring her to Roger's apartment. Roger has been struggling to write a song for a year, but finally finds the clichés that have eluded him for so long and sings them to the dying Mimi: "I have always loved you. / You can see it in my eyes." Mimi dies. But wait: her fever breaks; she lives—brought back to life by Roger's song.

When the small-scale production at the New York Theater Workshop on East Fourth Street in the East Village moved uptown to Broadway's Nederlander Theater on 41st Street, a move from a 150-seat venue to one with 1,173 seats, the *New York Times* theater critic said the play seemed "lost in space." The problem of scale that attaches to what was originally a small-scale production is only compounded by the techniques of modern cinema, with its wide-angle shots, long shots, dolly shots, and more. The big-budget resources required to transform an intimate theater production into blockbuster entertainment for a mass audience is at odds with the material: the commercial medium works against the cultural message.

At the same time, however much the bourgeois medium of mass entertainment conflicts with the bohemian material, that material is already "bourgeoisified" because it is so far removed from the actual East Village art scene in 1980s New York. The best way of making this point is the contrast of the music in the film with contemporary music at the time when the film is set. *Rent* puts the antics of its imaginary bohemians to the tune of an eclectic score that includes pop, garage-band grunge, sanitized punk, and show tunes in the Stephen Sondheim idiom (in fact, the lyrics of "La Vie de Bohème" name Sondheim as a bohemian hero). The score is a far cry from the music that one could hear in the 1980s at such legendary downtown venues as CBGB and the Cat Club or on the jukebox at Downtown Beirut, the bar not far from CBGB—the Ramones, Patti Smith, the Plastics, Tuxedomoon, Talking Heads, and many others. The real bohemian world of Alphabet City is long gone, of course, but anyone nostalgic for that world would be better served by Edo Bertoglio's *Downtown 81* (2000), shot in 1980–81 and featuring the artist Jean-Michel Basquiat.

This comparison of the real Alphabet City Bohemia with the fictional one the film evokes is somewhat unfair. After all, the historical reality of downtown New York in the 1980s is bound to seem more authentic than a 2005 film (*Rent*) based on a 1996 play (*Rent*) based on an 1896 opera (*La Bohème*) based on an 1849 play (*La vie de Bohême*) based on a collection of newspaper sketches published over the period 1845 to 1847. The film is at so many representational removes from the original that it cannot reliably offer a sense of historical reality. Or so it seems.

Here we need to recall that the myth of Bohemia was already well established in the 1840s when Murger fictionalized himself and his friends, so the historical reality is already mixed with fiction: story and history, like "bohemian" and "bourgeois" and other putative contraries, condition one another and make questions of originality and authenticity hard to answer. Indeed, Murger himself provided only provisional answers, perhaps because there is something about Bohemia itself that is provisional. As Murger said in the introduction to his 1851 book, "Bohemia is a stage in artistic life; it is the preface to the Academy, the Hôtel Dieu, or the Morgue." Does this mean that the only authentic bohemian is either sick or dead? Almost, since official acceptance by the French Academy (as happened in the case of Murger) hardly conforms to the concept of the vagabond bohemian living on the margins of society. But one thing is for sure: the history of Bohemia makes for a good story, and how good a story it makes depends on how much of the history we know.

Chapter 2
Historical Bohemias

George Sand may have imagined her fictional bohemians as residents of Venice and Florence without worrying too much about whether that fiction reflected historical reality. Besides, Sand's *The Last Aldini* understands Bohemia mainly as a condition, not a community. But starting with Balzac, fictional bohemians and historical bohemians walked the same streets—in Paris. Balzac's Prince of Bohemia, however, is not assigned a specific address. Yes, we are told that La Palférine saunters about, "cane in hand, up and down the pavement between the Rue de Grammont and the Rue de Richelieu," but we don't know where he lives, nor does he appear to be a member of a bohemian community whose denizens reside in a particular neighborhood. For the record, the streets where La Palférine strolls (especially the Rue de Richelieu) before he meets the dancer Claudine were in one of the more fashionable areas of Paris prior to the urban redesign that began in 1853: La Palférine begins his affair with Claudine on the Right Bank of the Seine (north of the river) in the second arrondissement, not far from the Paris stock exchange known as the Bourse. That is a long way—both geographically and culturally—from the more bohemian-friendly Latin Quarter on the Left Bank in the fifth arrondissement, or, for that matter, from those other neighborhoods that would become known as bohemian enclaves in later years—Montmartre and Montparnasse.

That later history follows from Baron Haussmann's redesign of Paris, with all the social redistribution the new design entailed, making some neighborhoods more respectable than others, with the poorest of the poor relegated to the banlieues on the periphery of the city. Prior to Haussmann's "horizontal" modifications of class distinctions in the new Paris, those distinctions were mostly "vertical," an effect, in part, of the medieval history of the city. Until Napoléon razed the last one, the succession of walls that ringed Paris meant that the only way to accommodate population growth was by building up, with most residents housed in multi-story dwellings (six or seven floors was typical). In the old Paris where Bohemia begins, a single house of multiple stories was often a microcosm of the broader society, the typical arrangement being a shop on the ground floor, with the shopkeeper lodging on the mezzanine level; then a bourgeois family on the second floor or *étage noble*, the "noble floor" (so called because it was removed from the noise and grime of the street but easily accessible up just one flight of stairs); the succeeding stories housed people progressively lower down on the income scale, with the most impoverished on the top floor.

In the cross-section of a typical Parisian house published in 1852, the ground floor is occupied by the concierge for the building. One flight up, the first floor shows a wealthy bourgeois couple relaxing in the *étage noble*, opulently decorated with wall sconces, drapery, and a chandelier (this apartment, unlike the others, has a balcony facing the street). The second floor is home to a family that includes two small children and an infant, as well as the mother of one of the proud parents; this family is less well-off than the couple on the first floor, but they are still comfortable, able to afford toys for the children and paintings for the wall. The third floor is divided into two apartments, one the residence of an older couple with a dog; they are poor but not utterly impoverished— they have two small pictures on the wall, also decorated with a cross. The other room on this floor is completely bare, the sole

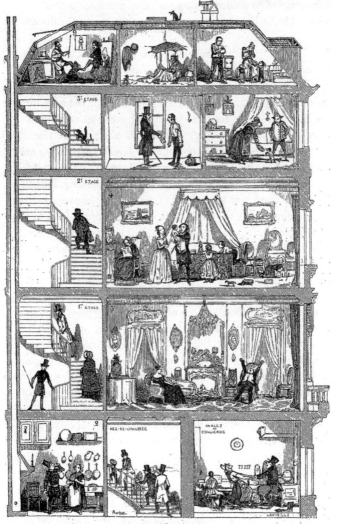

Cinq étages du monde parisien.

4. This cross-section of a typical Parisian house from the 1850s shows the wealthier families on the lower floors, with the more impoverished tenants higher up.

belongings of its occupant—who is being presented with a bill—evidently limited to the contents of the bag on the floor.

The top floor contains three tiny garret apartments, the square footage decreasing with the height above the street. In the small apartment facing the street we see a family of six, three small children clinging to the skirt of their mother, who holds an infant. The husband stands despondent, his arms crossed, no doubt wondering where his family's next meal is coming from. The middle apartment on this floor shows a derelict man sitting on a mattress on the floor, holding an umbrella to protect himself from the rain pouring through the leaky roof of the building. Finally, the garret apartment at the back of the building houses an artist, entertaining a male friend. With one painting on the wall, another on an easel, and several more on the floor leaning against the walls of the apartment, the two men appear to be quite happy, kicking up their heels and leading *la vie de bohème*.

Sand's fiction of Bohemia does not take adequate account of urban geography, and Balzac's misses the social history by making the Prince of Bohemia an isolated individual instead of a member of a community, but on both these points Henry Murger's *Scenes of Bohemian Life* accords with history. His fictional bohemians are not concentrated in a particular neighborhood—not even the Latin Quarter—but inevitably live on the top floor, or garret, of whatever house they can afford, regardless of neighborhood, an arrangement that reflects the urban reality of pre-Haussmann Paris. Despite the English title *Bohemians of the Latin Quarter*, whenever Murger mentions "le quartier Latine" (and there are only three such references), the context suggests that the bohemians are just passing through that neighborhood, as when Musette entertains in the Latin Quarter but then goes to her home in the Bréda district near Montmartre (the central hill—or butte—of Paris notable today for the basilica of Sacré-Coeur, started in 1875 but not completed until 1914).

At one point, when Rodolphe is trying to borrow rent money from his friends, he goes to see Schaunard, who is living in Montmartre, and when Schaunard fails to help, he tries Marcel, then residing in the rue de Bréda (now known as Rue Henry-Monnier). Early on, Colline and Rodolphe live at opposite ends of Paris, one on the Île Saint Louis, the other at Montmartre, but they and the other two bohemians celebrate their new friendship at a restaurant on the Rue Dauphine, which runs through the Latin Quarter. The next day, the bohemians begin the first of many meetings at the Café Momus. Even though in the first act of *La Bohème* Puccini has his bohemians sing, "Momus awaits us at the Latin Quarter" (Al Quartiere Latin ci attende Momus), the café was not, in fact, in the Latin Quarter at all. It was on the Right Bank, not far from the Louvre Museum (but easily accessible from the Latin Quarter across the Pont Neuf). The urban geography of Murger's *Scenes of Bohemian Life*, in short, suggests that the Latin Quarter was only one of several bohemian neighborhoods in the Paris of the 1840s.

The connection of bohemians to the Latin Quarter was already unraveling by Murger's time, but the association of that neighborhood with bohemian life had begun roughly two decades earlier, before *bohemian* had been invented as a term describing the life of the vagabond artist. Members of this earlier group called themselves by a succession of names: *le petit cénacle*, *le camp des Tartares*, *les jeunes France*, and, finally, *Bouzingos*. A *cénacle* (from Latin *cēnāculum*, "dining room") has various ecclesiastical meanings, including the room where the apostles gathered after the ascension of Christ. In French cultural history, the term was adopted to refer to a literary group with a clear leader, but not necessarily one with Christ-like qualities. The *petit cénacle* was a deliberate counter to the *grand cénacle* that formed around the critic Sainte-Beuve (pen name of Joseph Delorme) and Victor Hugo, whose anti-classicist play *Hernani* (1830), initially controversial but ultimately accepted, certified the success of the French Romantic movement.

Hernani marked a new phase of that movement, as the veneration of nature that the philosophy of Jean-Jacques Rousseau encouraged modulated into opposition to the hidebound rules of French *classicisme*. The move was Rousseuistic because Romantic resistance to the rules assured that literary expression could now be more "natural." After 1830, the "battle of *Hernani*" having been won, Hugo decamped from the Latin Quarter for the Place Royale (now Place de Vosges), a more respectable neighborhood, even as his former disciples became more anti-bourgeois than anti-classical. Many of Hugo's admirers who had been part of the *grand cénacle*, such as the all-round literary man Théophile Gautier (poet, novelist, playwright, critic, journalist) and the poet Gerard de Nerval, stayed around for the *petit* version.

This *cénacle* was led for a while by the less well-known Pétrus Borel, who started out as a poet but ended as a bureaucrat in French colonial Algeria. Borel seems to have been responsible for the name *Tartares*, that is, Tartars or Tatars, the name given to the fearsome Turkic-speaking nomads of Central Asia felt to be a threat to civilized Europe. No doubt for Borel and others in the group the name connoted a savage challenge to bourgeois society, whereas *Jeunes France* (Young France) implied not the destruction of civilization so much as its renewal by means of Romantic culture. As for *Bouzingos* (sometimes spelled *Bouzingots*), the name is of uncertain etymology: it may refer to a type of leather hat worn by sailors or to "noise makers," *bousin* being one French word for "noise." Either way, the word seems to have been deliberately concocted as a contrast to *bourgeois*. Interestingly, the basic senses of all these names—*Tartares, Jeunes France, Bouzingos*—are readily subsumed by the term *bohémiens*—a small group of young, noisy French savages antagonistic to the established society of their times.

Historically, then, Murger and his fellows belonged to the second or third wave of Parisian bohemians, depending on whether the *grand cénacle* counts or not, since that group antedates the widespread use of the term *bohémiens*. In some ways, the urban geography recorded in Murger's book harkens back to the neighborhood favored by the first bohemians who were named as such even as it looks forward to the preferred region of future bohemians. That earlier Bohemia is evoked by the Right Bank neighborhood near the Louvre where the Café Momus stood, while those to come are implied by the areas where Shaunard and Colline find low-rent lodging—in and around Montmartre.

The first bohemians congregated at several addresses on the Impasse du Doyenné, a derelict dead-end street, and the street that intersected it, the Rue du Doyenné (neither street exists today). This Right Bank neighborhood was near the Place du Carrousel, opposite the Jardin des Tuileries, a couple minutes walk from the Louvre. Gautier, having transferred his "membership" from the pre- to the post-1830 Romantics, described the neighborhood in a way that was consistent with the bohemian sensibility of the times: "The Impasse ends in a plot of closed ground, sectioned off by a fence made from planks salvaged from boats and blackened by time. The ruins of a church . . . helped make the place seem wild and sinister. . . . There a small colony of artists, a band of picturesque, literary bohemians led a Robinson Crusoe life . . . in the middle of Paris, opposite the constitutional and bourgeois monarchy." The reference to Robinson Crusoe is a reminder of the Anglophilia of many French Romantics (reflected in Murger's first-name change from Henri to Henry), but it mainly suggests that Gautier and his friends thought of their neighborhood as a bohemian island in a bourgeois sea.

Like Gautier, Nerval also found his way to the bohemian community at the Impasse du Doyenné, joined by the future critic Arsène Houssaye, the illustrator Paul Gavarni, and the painters Camille Corot and Eugène Delacroix. Not all of these men were residents of the Impasse but came and went, often taking advantage of the hospitality of the painter Camille Rogier, who lived across from Gautier. In a book with the delightful title *Petits*

Nerval on the Impasse du Doyenné

It was in our shared place on La Rue de Doyenné, in a corner of the old Louvre of the Médicis and very close to the spot where the old Hôtel de Rambouillet once stood, that we came to know each other as brothers. . . .

The doyen's old living room, with the four swinging doors and the ceiling that was elaborately decorated with *rocailles* and dragon designs—restored by the labors of so many painters, our friends, who have since become famous—resounded with our gallant rhymes, which were often interspersed with joyous laughter or the mad songs of the Cydalises.

The good Rogier was laughing into his beard from the top of a ladder, where he was painting a Neptune (who looked just like him!). . . . Suddenly, the two swinging doors crashed open: it was Théophile. We scrambled to fetch him a Louis XIII armchair and in turn he read his first verses, while the first Cydalise, or Lorry, or Victorine, swung nonchalantly in the hammock belonging to the fair-haired Sarah, which was suspended across the immense living room.

Occasionally, one of us would get up and dream of new verses while looking out from the windows upon the sculpted façades of the museum's gallery, animated from this side by the trees of the carousel. . . .

What happy times! We threw balls, dinners, costume parties. We put on old plays, where mademoiselle Plessy, who was still a debutante, did not decline to accept a role—that of Beatrice in *Jodelet*. And our poor Edouard was hilarious in the Harlequin parts!

We were young, always merry, and often rich. But I just struck a somber note: our palace was demolished. Last autumn, I walked over its debris.

—Gerard Nerval, *Petits châteaux de bohême* (1853)

châteaux de bohême (Little bohemian castles, 1853), Nerval provides a rich description of bohemian life in Rogier's "castle." Some details Nerval recalls might be hard to parse today, like the reference to "mademoiselle Plessy," later known as the actress Madame Jeanne Sylvanie Arnould-Plessy, and to *Jodelet* (1645), a comedy by Paul Scarron. "La Cydalise" is the name Rogier gave to his mistress, which Nerval makes plural, suggesting the appellation might refer to any bohemian goddess (the real name of the woman called La Cydalise is unknown, but she is said to have been a seamstress who died of tuberculosis, like Puccini's Mimì).

Nerval is known today as an influential figure in French literature whose fantastic poetry points toward surrealism even as some of his outlandish activities, if true, suggest an early form of Dada performance. Gautier tells a story about Nerval and his pet lobster, which he would take for walks, leading the crustacean by a blue silk ribbon, in the neighborhood of the Palais-Royale. Nerval is supposed to have justified his actions by claiming that having a lobster for a pet was "no more ridiculous" than having a dog—"or a cat, or a gazelle, or a lion, or any other animal that we take for walks. I have a liking for lobsters. They are peaceful, serious creatures who know the secrets of the sea, they don't bark, and they don't invade your privacy like dogs do. After all, Goethe was averse to dogs, and he wasn't mad!"

Gautier's lobster anecdote was long thought to be apocryphal, as any number of basic facts suggest (lobsters are aquatic, and the difference between their terrestrial footspeed and that of the person leading them by a leash suggests dragging rather than walking). But some of Nerval's letters appear to confirm it, so the question arises as to whether the poet's bizarre behavior means he was acting as a bohemian out to *épater la bourgeoisie* (shock the bourgeoisie) or was, unlike Goethe, quite mad.

Another of Nerval's contemporaries confesses to being a bit worried about his friend when he learns that the poet has been engaging in conversations with the goldfish in a pond at the Jardin de Tuileries. This incident, like the one involving the lobster, proved to be diagnostic: Nerval had a nervous breakdown in 1841 and was in and out of mental institutions thereafter, becoming increasingly destitute, forced to live the vagabond life of a bohemian artist in all-too-literal terms as a homeless man on the streets of Paris. In 1855 he committed suicide on one of them—the rue de la Vielle-Lanterne—by hanging himself from a window grating. Nerval's story shows that some bohemians really do live on the edge, and those who do not "graduate" from Bohemia into proper society, as Hugo and Murger did, run some very real risks.

The street where Nerval killed himself—on the Right Bank near the Île de la Cité—no longer exists, destroyed as part of Haussmann's renovation of Paris. The rue de la Vielle-Lanterne is—or was—about a fifteen-minute walk from the next major site of bohemian life in nineteenth-century Paris: the Hôtel Pimodan (now the Hôtel Lauzun) on the Île Saint-Louis, built in the seventeenth century. Among the bohemians who were attracted to the old *hôtel*, or private mansion, were the Gothic novelist Roger de Beauvoir, the painter Fernand Boissard, and, of course, Gautier—whose career runs through all of the Bohemias of the Romantic era. Beauvoir was such a slave to fashion that he wore different colored gloves depending on the time of day, which prompted one Parisian wit to say that he must suffer from "chronic elegantiasis." Boissard was key to the formation of the *Club des Hachichins* (Club of the hashish eaters) that met once a month at the Hôtel Pimodan from 1845 to 1849. In 1845 Boissard sent Gautier an invitation beginning, "My dear Théophile, hashish will be taken at my house, Monday, September 3rd.... Do you want to participate?" Boissard promised Gautier that he could be assured of "hallucination," but that if he was "afraid of impure contacts, I think I can suggest a method of isolation, the hotel Pimodan makes it possible."

Boissard's concern about "impure contacts" is probably an ironic dig at Gautier for becoming too successful and respectable to be regarded as a true bohemian. In any event, Gautier fictionalized his experiences taking hashish at the Hôtel Pimodan in "Le Club des Hachichins," published in February 1846 in the prestigious *Revue des Deux Mondes*. In it, he describes the experience of taking hashish in some detail: "Then, suddenly, a red flash passed under my eyelids, and I felt myself bathed in a warm, golden light.... [E]verything was larger, richer, more splendid. Reality served only as the point of departure for the magnificence of the hallucination." Alcohol consumption was typical of earlier bohemian gatherings, but regular drug use seems to have been an innovation of the Pimodan group that would have a long and continuing history.

The most important bohemian resident of the Hôtel Pimodan was Charles Baudelaire, who moved to the top floor of the building in 1843 and decorated his apartment in lavish style, the most striking feature being the broad red and black stripes of the wallpaper. Only twenty-two at the time, the future author of *Les fleurs du mal* (*The Flowers of Evil*, 1857) was flush with cash, an inheritance from his father (who died in 1827) that had been withheld until he reached the age of twenty-one. Baudelaire had consorted with bohemians as a student, so much so that when he was twenty his mother and stepfather sought to reform him by sending him to India, believing that he would find more wholesome inspiration for his poetry on the subcontinent than in "the sewers of Paris."

He made it as far as the French colonial islands of Mauritius and Réunion off Madagascar but refused to go any farther. Back in Paris, he received his inheritance and started a short-lived spending spree, mostly on books and clothes. Personal wealth and a bohemian lifestyle are not necessarily incompatible, but Baudelaire did not have a chance to test that theory in full. Alarmed at the accumulation of debt, his family took legal measures to remove the money from his control. Starting in 1844 and until the end of his life, Baudelaire had his inheritance doled out to him in small amounts by the family lawyer, acting as trustee. Hence Baudelaire was "free" to pursue the bohemian life from the mid-1840s on.

But he did not. Baudelaire is an important transitional figure in many ways. In broad cultural terms, his poetry moves from the relatively straightforward, emotive self-expression of Romanticism to the more psychologically complex style of modernism. In social terms, Baudelaire traverses several identities, moving from bohemian to dandy to decadent. In addition to his many other roles, the ubiquitous Gautier appears as a kind of Baudelaire whisperer for his remarkable ability to assess the poet's place in the shifting culture and evolving society of mid-nineteenth-century France. Hence it is significant that, after meeting Baudelaire at the Hôtel Pimodan in the summer 1843, Gautier remarked of him that "[o]ne might say he was a dandy who had strayed into Bohemia, but kept his rank and manners and that cult of self which is typical of the man imbued with the principles of Brummel." The reference is to George Bryan Brummel, the British socialite who established the new urban mode of fashion known as dandyism, a form of dress more elegant than flamboyant (at least at the beginning). Equally important, however, is the manner of the dandy as someone reserved to the point of aloofness. The dandy, in short, imagines himself as a cultural aristocrat, and while there is no shortage of real aristocrats slumming as bohemians, neither the economic nor the social status of the aristocracy accords with the down-market myth of Bohemia.

Here it is worth noting that Baudelaire begins the transition away from Bohemia to cultivate other artistic and social identities at more or less the same time that Murger begins to chronicle his own bohemian adventures and those of his friends. Baudelaire met Murger and the other members of the group sometime in the late 1840s, and it is perhaps telling that the poet does not appear to have a fictional counterpart in *Scenes of Bohemian Life* even though, after 1844, his bohemian "qualifications" had been renewed when he lost control of his inheritance. A story about Baudelaire and Alexandre Schanne, the original of Schaunard, offers an ambiguous image of bohemian life. Baudelaire invited Schanne to dine with him, but when Schanne arrived the poet provided only a plate of Brie and a couple of bottles of Bordeaux. The wine and cheese served as the dessert after the dinner, which Baudelaire asked Schanne to imagine since no main course had been provided. It is hard to tell from the anecdote whether Baudelaire was behaving as a bohemian in fact or simply adopting the pose of the destitute poet to entertain his bohemian friend. However ambiguous the story seems, there can be no doubt that as his career progressed Baudelaire had less and less to do with the likes of bohemians like Schanne.

But another factor in Baudelaire's removal from Bohemia may well have been the removal of Bohemia itself from the realm of urban experience. Given Haussmann's rapid modernization of the city, Paris became less amenable to bohemian possibilities as low-rent neighborhoods were replaced by upscale enclaves where the bourgeois, commercial class could live and work. Baudelaire described the transformation of Paris in "Le Cygne" ("The Swan"), a poem that allegorizes the poet's disillusionment—and discomfort—with the new Paris as a great white swan stumbling over the paving stones of a new boulevard, trailing its pure white feathers in the filth of the street. "The old Paris is gone," the poet says, and while "Paris may change," he does not. Like the swan removed from its element, the poet is an exile in his own city.

Baudelaire's "The Swan" first appeared in the second edition of *The Flowers of Evil* in 1861, so the poet's lament about "old Paris" ceasing to exist reflects the reality of the accelerated pace of the Haussmann modernization that began in 1860. In 1863 Baudelaire described the social changes he was living through as "décadence," a period of transition "when democracy is not yet all-powerful, and aristocracy is only just beginning to totter and fall." During such times, Baudelaire chose to ally himself not with the bohemians but with the dandies (recalling Gautier's earlier assessment of the poet's true character), claiming that, "Dandyism is the last spark of heroism amid decadence." When Baudelaire died in 1867, he died as a dandy, his work regarded by succeeding generations as an expression of *décadence*, not *bohémianisme*. The temptation is to say that historical Bohemia comes to a close just as fictional Bohemia begins to take off as a mixture of mythic character types and cultural conventions. But historical Bohemia does *not* end with the popularity of fictional Bohemia in the middle of the nineteenth century—it continues for some time to come, history having received fresh impetus from myth.

A good example of the way myth inspires history is the group that congregated at Pfaff's saloon in downtown New York in the late 1850s, the earliest of several New York Bohemias. In 1853, the *Knickerbocker Magazine* began the serial publication of Murger's book in a translation by Carl Benson using the title *The Gypsies of Art*. Around the same time as the *Knickerbocker* serialization, Henry Clapp Jr., a New York journalist who had spent three years in Paris experiencing the café culture of that city first-hand, adopted the bohemian identity and tried to recreate his Parisian experiences in downtown Manhattan. A man of considerable wit and charisma, Clapp soon became known as the "King of Bohemia" at Pfaff's, the basement bar at 653 Broadway, near Bleecker Street, owned and operated by a German immigrant named Charles I. Pfaff.

The place included a room that extended under the sidewalk known as "the vault," where Clapp held forth. In October 1858 he began publication of the *Saturday Press*, a deliberately bohemian venture whose historical importance was assured once Clapp began promoting the work of Walt Whitman in its pages. All told, Clapp published more than forty pieces either by or about Whitman from 1859 to 1861, including an early version of "Out of

5. Walt Whitman adopted the relaxed, informal pose of the bohemian for the frontispiece to the first edition of *Leaves of Grass* (1855), his epoch-making book of poetry.

the Cradle Endlessly Rocking," one of the poet's best-known poems. He also printed the advertisement for the 1860 edition of Whitman's *Leaves of Grass* some thirty-five times, all of which prompted Whitman to tell his biographer that "my own history could not be written with Henry left out."

Although Whitman revised his persona multiple times over his long career, during the period of his association with Clapp he considered himself a bohemian, as his unfinished poem "The Two Vaults" (ca. 1861–62) shows:

> The vault at Pfaffs where the drinkers and laughers meet to eat and
>   drink and carouse
> While on the walk immediately overhead pass the myriad feet of
>   Broadway
> As the dead in their graves are underfoot hidden
> And the living pass over them, recking not of them,
> Laugh on laughers!
> Drink on drinkers!

The title of the poem contrasts the vault at Pfaff's with a burial vault, implying that, ironically, those hurrying about above ground are less alive than the revelers below.

The New York Bohemia was to be short-lived, largely because the Civil War (1861–65) forced on Americans an unprecedented need for duty and commitment. But even before the war, the *New York Times* cautioned its readers about the dangers of "Bohemianism":

> There has long been a tribe of loose subjects living in Paris, who have been denominated Bohemians; not because they spring from Bohemia, but owing to their habits of life being of that loose and desultory nature peculiar to the Gipsy [*sic*] tribe....In a great city like New-York, where there must be a constant overflow of talent from the learned professions Bohemianism receives largely accessions from the bar and the medical college. Unemployed

doctors, and blighted lawyers who have a taste for music, for the fine arts, or for poetry, become Bohemians by the most natural process possible, and once they fall into the ways of the tribe, they are lost forever. A young man may rise from a lower plane of social existence, and while in a transition state may mingle for a while in the rabble rout of Bohemians, and not be made the worse for it; but the man who descends to them is lost irretrievably.

The *Times* correspondent added that, even though bohemianism "is the inevitable product of a great city,... the Bohemian cannot be called a useful member of society."

In 1865, after the war, Clapp tried to restart the *Saturday Press*, which ceased publication in 1861, but the second iteration of the newspaper soon foundered in the face of a changed American society that required its members to be even more useful than before. As the staid establishment novelist William Dean Howells said of the Pfaff group in 1900, "It was in fact but a sickly colony, transplanted from the mother asphalt of Paris, and never really striking root in the pavements of New York."

Howells was right to understand Bohemia as a product of French history and Parisian culture that would not take root as readily in the New World as it had in the Old. This despite the fact that another American (in addition to Clapp) had attained the status of "King of Bohemia" among French intellectuals. That epithet had been conferred on Edgar Allan Poe in 1856 by the novelist Jules Barbey d'Aurevilly, who also said that Poe was "Bohemia raised to the highest power" because his artistic greatness towered above the mundane interests of his compatriots, making him "the cream of the scum of the earth." But Poe was an isolated figure, and a single individual does not a bohemian community make.

After Pfaff's, the next collection of American bohemians would be found in San Francisco, even though the group was not so much a community as a club—and its members may not have really been bohemians. In 1872, a group of local journalists, led by James F. Bowman of the San Francisco *Chronicle* and Daniel O'Connell of the *Bulletin*, founded the Bohemian Club to promote "good fellowship among journalists, and the elevation of journalism to that place in the popular estimation to which it is entitled." Initially, then, the Bohemian Club was little more than a trade association that served alcohol, but after a spirited debate (which included discussion of Henry Murger's *Scenes of Bohemian Life*) membership was extended to include actors, playwrights, poets, and artists. At first, newspaper owners were barred from the club, but in succeeding years professionals and businessmen of all stripes could pay the membership fee and so become "bohemians." One of the draws of membership was the annual bacchanal known as the High Jinks, a festival of music, drama, and drinking held at the Bohemian Grove, a campground in the redwood forests outside San Francisco. The all-male club is still in existence today.

The High Jinks in the Bohemian Grove suggests an idea of Bohemia that is not so different from a corporate retreat. What makes the San Francisco phenomenon such a departure from the bohemian tradition is the embrace of the bourgeoisie. True, the line between the bohemian and the bourgeois sometimes seems a bit fuzzy, but the blurring results from some real social tension between the two. The Bohemian Club did not resolve that tension but simply dismissed it—by "rebranding" the bourgeois gentleman a bohemian enthusiast. The San Franciscans also departed from bohemian tradition by abandoning the city for the countryside as a place to stage their (temporary) rebellion against social conventions.

This pastoral preference is not so unusual in the annals of American bohemians, however much it may depart from the urban prototype of Paris. Howells called the Pfaff's group a "colony," meaning that the New York Bohemia was a colonial outpost of the Parisian original. In the United States, the colonial model underwent a further development when urban bohemians congregated in the countryside and formed communities geographically separate from but culturally identical to their metropolitan base. A good example of the phenomenon is the dual Bohemia that formed prior to World War I in New York's Greenwich Village and Provincetown, Massachusetts, on the coast of Cape Cod (one member of this double Bohemia called Provincetown "Greenwich Village sunburnt").

But not all of the bohemian communities in America had a home base in a major city. An example is the Maverick Art Colony of Woodstock, New York, which, despite the name, was located in the nearby township of West Hurley. Founded in 1905 by Hervey White, a poet and novelist who admired the British socialist John Ruskin, the Maverick colony illustrates the convergence of two different strains in American experience: bohemian culture and utopian community. One of the most persistent themes in U.S. history is the rejection of mainstream society as too crass and commercial to satisfy the spiritual needs of certain individuals, who isolate themselves from the larger world by forming a separate, ideal community. Examples include Mount Lebanon, the Shaker society founded in 1787 in New Lebanon, New York; Brook Farm, the Transcendentalist community organized in 1841 outside Roxbury, Massachusetts; and the anarchist Ferrer Colony established in 1915 in Stelton, New Jersey.

Despite differences in these communities—some religious, some secular—they all had a similar utopian purpose: "to prepare a society of liberal, intelligent, and cultivated persons, whose relations with each other would permit a more simple and wholesome life, than can be led amidst the pressure of competitive institutions." That is the way the founder of Brook Farm summed up his goals, which also works as description of artist colonies like the Maverick. Nonetheless, such colonies do not figure prominently in histories of Bohemia, mainly because of their utopian removal from society at large. Like the Bohemian Club of

San Francisco, they do not exist in tension with the bourgeoisie, but for a different reason. Bohemians define themselves in opposition to the bourgeoisie—artistically, socially, and morally—something that is difficult to do if there are no bourgeoisie around. A colony is not a neighborhood. The city, in short, provides opportunity and occasion for bohemian experience in ways that the countryside does not.

In Germany, Munich emerged as the city most conducive to bohemian culture at the turn of the century, when the country began the transition from a backward empire to a modern nation-state. The poet Stefan George, like Baudelaire (a major influence), was preoccupied with cultural transition, or *Übergang* (literally, "crossing over"), and he—like Baudelaire—understood the idea of transition as closely connected to the idea of decadence, or *Untergang* (literally, "going under," or "downfall"). But whereas Baudelaire had a rich national heritage on which to base his choice of artistic direction (including *la Bohême*), George did not. The independent states and hereditary dominions of the Holy Roman Empire, the Hapsburg monarchy, and other political entities combined into the nation of Germany only after the Franco-Prussian War ended in 1871. Hence, in Germany debates about national culture were only just beginning, whereas in France those debates, while not exactly settled, had longstanding cultural traditions behind them. The idea of Bohemia is a case in point: its place in the national culture of France seems secure today, partly because of its relationship to the Romantic tradition. That relationship, in fact, may be one reason that Baudelaire gravitated away from Bohemia as his own poetic imagination and cultural preoccupations developed in the direction of what we now call modernism.

Stefan George, on the other hand, tended toward Bohemia, but a Bohemia infused less with Romanticism and more with decadence. Indeed, the perennially nomadic German poet actually "shopped around" for the kind of urban environs most favorable to the decadent life of art he wished to live. George was thoroughly familiar with Paris, but since he was born in 1868 (the year after Baudelaire died), the Paris he knew was well removed from the old city so conducive to the bohemian life of a bygone era. Nonetheless, the French influence was insistent for George in other ways. For a while, he fashioned himself almost as a French poet writing in German (in standard German, all nouns are capitalized, but in George's poetic German they are not—hence his poetry has the "look" of French).

In addition to being influenced by Baudelaire, he was also profoundly affected by the French symbolist poet Stéphane Mallarmé, whose often opaque poetry, attuned more to nuance and mood than to meaning, George sought to emulate. But however much Mallarmé may have influenced George's work, the French poet was no model for George's life, for there was nothing bohemian about Mallarmé, who led a modest, stable life as an English teacher and jobbing journalist. As he began to distance himself from France and remake himself as a kind of poet-priest, a cultural prophet of the new Germany, George settled on the Bavarian city of Munich, which had several advantages over the commercial metropolis of Berlin. Urban planners had redesigned the city along Hellenistic, neoclassical lines during the reign of the Wittelsbach king Ludwig I (r. 1825–48), transforming the Bavarian capital into "Athens on the Isar" (Berlin, by contrast, would come to be known as "Sodom on the Spree"), a *Kunststadt* or "city of art." Another advantage Munich held for George and his followers was the availability of inexpensive housing: rents were low because supply exceeded demand, thanks to the exodus of workers to the industrial mecca of Berlin and other Prussian cities.

Still another appeal was the class makeup of the city: "Munich is the only city on earth without 'the bourgeois,'" he wrote to a friend, "here there is only the *Volk* and the youth." George surely overstates the case, since Munich includes several neighborhoods designed to house the bourgeoisie, but what he says is mostly true of the neighborhood of Schwabing, which had supported a thriving bohemian community well before George settled there. Home to several universities, including the Academy of Fine Arts, the area had a combination of student populations and low-rent housing that provided the same kind of bohemian-friendly environment as the Latin Quarter and other Paris neighborhoods. This milieu led later writers to refer to the area as the "Bavarian Montmartre" and "Schwabylon," the latter term suggesting that the city of art was also a city of sin (like ancient Babylon). Among the many writers, artists, and political figures resident in Schwabing at the turn of the century were the Mann bothers, Thomas and Heinrich; the poet Rainer Maria Rilke; the playwright Frank Wedekind; the novelist Fanny "Franziska" zu Reventlow (known as the Bohemian Countess of Schwabing); the painters Wassily Kandinsky and Paul Klee; the anarchist Erich Mühsam; and the future leader of the Russian Revolution, Vladimir Ilyich Lenin.

Not all of these figures conformed to the mythic "starving artist" mold of Bohemia—far from it, in fact. For all his antipathy to the bourgeoisie, George was allowed the freedom to dedicate himself to the life of art by his bourgeois father, who had made a modest fortune as a wine merchant. And the Bohemian countess was a countess in fact, her aristocratic lineage evident in her fantastically full name, Fanny Liane Wilhelmine Sophie Auguste Adrienne Gräfin zu Reventlow. The sexually liberated Reventlow left her husband to study art and pursue a writing career, taking many lovers along the way and never naming the man who fathered her son. She was the only woman in the mostly homosocial and partly homosexual salon of Schwabing bohemians known as the *Kosmikerkreis*, or "Cosmic Circle," a group led by George that debated the future of German culture in highly elevated terms, as the name Cosmic Circle suggests (the term was inspired by the philosophy of Friedrich Nietzsche, whom the group understood to be a new, superior type of person, a *Kosmiker Mensch*, or "Cosmic Man").

George Sand notwithstanding, very few women have had roles in bohemian circles outside those of model or mistress. So Reventlow stands out, not only for her association with the Schwabing Bohemia but also for her creative contributions to it. Given this fact, it is somewhat surprising to find the rather ostentatiously liberated Reventlow taking anti-feminist positions. In "Viragines oder Hetären?" (Viragos or hetaerae?, 1899; *virago* means "bitch," *hetaera* "mistress"), Reventlow presented promiscuity as a positive value threatened by feminist arguments for political empowerment: "As long as the women's movement tries to make women manly it is the decided enemy of any erotic culture."

Later, she recounted her experiences with the Cosmic Circle in *Herrn Dames Aufzeichnungen; oder Begebenheiten aus einem merkwürdigen Stadtteil* (Mister Dame's records; or events from a curious quarter, 1913), a roman à clef (Reventlow herself provided the key to the novel) that describes the activities of the group in detail, such as a Carnival celebration that took place in February 1903. The role of Dionysus was taken by Karl Wolfskehl, George's most devoted acolyte and a reliable source of financial support (he was the son of a wealthy banker), while George himself appeared as Caesar.

The "matron" at this celebration was a rather unhinged neo-pagan named Alfred Schuler, who appeared in black drag as Magna Mater or "Great Mother," a fertility goddess whose rites achieved widespread popularity during the reign of the decadent Roman emperor Elagabalus (r. 218–22), the subject also of *Algabal* (1892), one of George's collections of lyric poetry.

Despite their high-minded intentions, the Schwabing bohemians unfortunately prefigure another Munich group that formed in

Reventlow on the Schwabing Bohemia

The saturnalia began with a solemn procession: a bacchante, beating a metal cymbal, went in front, then came Dionysus with his golden staff, followed by Caesar—he carried a sort of spherical, perforated jar with a light burning inside it—and the matron, dressed all in black, while boys holding wine goblets wreathed around between them. Those dressed in antique garb followed, with others standing to one side. Quite a few wore different costumes—Renaissance, Teutonic, Oriental.... Then everything dissolved into animated chaos, with dancing and the usual rites practiced at such feasts. I recall a colorful blur of individual images and impressions that I would like to capture before they fade away....

But now the priest seized the gong and entered the arena. With booming blows and a sinister face he stepped up to the dancer and spurred her on to attempt even wilder movements. She received tremendous applause, her red veils swirling up and down. I finally felt as if I were hypnotized, unable to see or feel anything but red veils, red veils—or hear anything but the clanging of the gong. Perhaps this was indeed the Dionysian state of intoxication this celebration was supposed to induce....

The dancer was still dancing, she seemed unable to stop—when suddenly the priest tossed the gong aside and began to spin round and round like a dervish. This gave the signal for everyone to descend into ecstasy, everyone started to dance, to swirl, to gyrate at a frantic tempo: in pairs, alone, or in groups—whatever. An entire swarm of maenads swayed in a circle around Dionysus, who with enraptured gaze looked now at one, now another, and tried to catch them.

—Fanny zu Reventlow, *Herrn Dames Aufzeichnungen* (1913)

1920: the National Socialist Party led by Adolf Hitler. The Nazis recognized in George one of the prophets of the new Germany, an impression that George's last book, *Das Neue Reich* (*The New Reich*, 1928), appears to certify (even though the poems in it do not concern a political realm so much as a mystical one that mediates body and spirit). Reventlow was an early advocate of the "healthy pleasure" of nudity, anticipating the Nazi encouragement of physical culture, and the neo-pagan Schuler is credited with the promotion of the design motif that originated in India and appeared on Greek pottery and Roman mosaics: the swastika.

What are we to make of such developments? Do the disturbing currents in German culture manifested by the Schwabing bohemians mean that the politics of the group is unsettling only in the light of later history? Or do the proto-Nazi elements in the *Kosmikerkreis* argue for an ugly continuity between the aesthetics

6. Fanny zu Reventlow reveals that her promotion of nudity as a healthy bohemian pleasure was not just theoretical.

of the group and the awful ideology to come? Whatever the answer, the relationship between culture and politics in the case of the Schwabing Bohemia seems to say something about the bohemian tradition more generally: that its capacity to accommodate seemingly conflicting social trajectories—the downwardly mobile bourgeoisie looking for a good time and the upwardly mobile artist or writer seeking establishment acceptance—might also accommodate other kinds of conflicts, including the combination of progressive art and regressive ideology. For example, when Gautier was engaged in a literary revolution as a young bohemian living on the Impasse du Doyenné, he had no interest in republican ideals. "The two greatest things in the world," he wrote in 1834, are "royalty and poetry."

Murger may not have been quite so revolutionary a writer as Gautier, but he, too, was hardly a man of the people. For a while Murger worked as secretary for an obscure Russian émigré in Paris, one Count Tolstoy (Jacques, not the better-known Leo), supplying the Count with information in the lead-up to the 1848 rebellion, which the Count incorporated into his reports to the tsar. Technically speaking, such activity made Murger a political spy working on behalf of counterrevolutionary powers, even though he was just doing the job for the money. Still, the political posture he took at the time hardly argues for bohemians as culture warriors for the left. In the nineteenth century, there are only a handful of exceptions to the general rule that bohemians are less than progressive and remain, at best, apolitical. The fictional hero of George Sand's *The Last Aldini* did express allegiance to republican ideals, but it would not be until the early twentieth century that history would catch up to fiction by allying bohemian culture with progressive ideology.

Chapter 3
Political Bohemias

Bohemians and Marxists both abhor the bourgeoisie, which would seem to make the two groups ideological allies. But Karl Marx himself had scant interest in the political potential of bohemians and even used the term "bohemian" as a slur when he referred to Napoléon III, of all people, as a "bohemian, a princely lumpenproletariat." *Lumpenproletariat* combines a form of the Latin word *prōlētārius* (the lowest class of Roman citizens) with the German word for "rag," *Lumpen*, and refers, in Marx's vocabulary, to those workers who are so degraded they cannot be organized for purposes of collective action. The word is roughly equivalent to "ragpicker," which in its French form as *chiffonnier* was well known in nineteenth-century Paris as a street "profession"—one that Baudelaire memorialized in his poem "Le vin de chiffonniers" ("The Ragman's Wine").

The "princely lumpenproletariat" epithet perhaps goes some way toward explaining just how amorphous and indeterminate bohemian politics tends to be, since bohemians—at least in the nineteenth century—formed themselves into artistic communities that could conceivably include members of different social classes. The example of Fanny zu Reventlow in turn-of-the-century Schwabing shows that bohemian circles were hardly closed to the aristocracy. Perhaps the mongrel nature of bohemian communities was something Marx objected to because multiple class identifications worked against the grain of his political philosophy, which required different social classes to maintain a measure of ideological clarity and stay in their designated political lanes. After all, how could the class struggle occur if the urban poor, slumming aristocrats, and bourgeois, weekend bohemians were not struggling against one another in fact but meeting for drinks in the same café?

Whatever the motivation, Marx's jaundiced opinion of bohemians deserves a closer look for the obvious reason that no political philosopher in the nineteenth century made more effort than Marx did to understand the social makeup of the bourgeoisie, the very class against which most bohemians define themselves. The startling identification of Napoléon III as a "bohemian" appears in Marx's *The Eighteenth Brumaire of Louis Bonaparte*, a pamphlet first published in a German-language magazine in New York in 1852. Marx was living in London but followed developments in France closely; indeed, *The Eighteenth Brumaire* is a near-contemporary account of the coup d'état of December 1851 whereby Louis-Napoléon Bonaparte refused to accept the term limits of his office as President of the Second Republic (1848–52) and engineered the government takeover that established him as Napoléon III, Emperor of the Second Empire (1852–70).

Marx understands this second Napoléon as a poor substitute for the first, in keeping with his withering assessment at the very beginning of the pamphlet: "Hegel observes somewhere that all the great events and characters of world history occur twice, so to speak. He forgot to add: the first time as high tragedy, the second time as low farce." The title *The Eighteenth Brumaire* refers to the date on the French Republican Calendar (adopted over the revolutionary years of 1793 to 1805) otherwise known as November 9, 1799, when the first Napoléon declared himself Emperor. That tragic date, in Marx's view, has December 2, 1851, as its farcical counterpart, when the supporters of Louis-Napoléon broke up the Legislative Assembly and paved his way to autocratic rule. Marx describes the new emperor's supporters as a band of "bohemians":

> Under the pretext of incorporating a benevolent association, the Paris lumpenproletariat was organised into secret sections, each led by a Bonapartist agent, and the whole headed by a Bonapartist general. From the aristocracy there were bankrupted roués of doubtful means and dubious provenance, from the bourgeoisie there were degenerate wastrels on the take, vagabonds, demobbed soldiers, discharged convicts, runaway galley slaves, swindlers and cheats, thugs, pickpockets, conjurers, card-sharps, pimps, brothel keepers, porters, day labourers, organ grinders, scrap dealers, knife grinders, tinkers and beggars, in short, the whole amorphous, jumbled mass of flotsam and jetsam that the French term bohemian....

The Eighteenth Brumaire appeared in the same year that Henry Murger published his newspaper sketches in book form as *Scenes of Bohemian Life*, and, given how attuned Marx was to cultural developments in France, he could have had Murger's bohemians in mind when he wrote his screed against Louis Bonaparte.

But a more likely explanation is that Marx had an earlier meaning in mind, the one based on the pejorative comparison of the itinerant lives of the Romany people from Bohemia to the hand-to-mouth, vagabond existence of Parisian street people who made a living any way they could, whether by begging for scraps of food or committing petty crimes. These types of bohemians were even further removed from bourgeois society than the would-be painters and poets whose stories Murger chronicled. But they too had their lives documented by a kind of Murger of the gutter named Alexandre Privat d'Anglemont, a noctambulist newspaperman whose familiarity with the most disreputable parts and persons of Paris was legendary.

Born in the French colony of Guadeloupe to a mixed-race woman and an unknown father, Privat's illegitimacy and racial makeup may have contributed to his affection for the extremely marginal Parisians whose lives and livelihoods he chronicled in two books, *Paris Anecdote* (1854) and *Paris Inconnu* (Unknown Paris, 1861). Alexandre Schanne, the model for Schaunard, called him "the arch-bohemian," that high cultural status further certified by a remark attributed to Murger, who is supposed to have told his friend, "You are not a bohemian, you are Bohemia." The title of Privat's second book, published posthumously by his friend and fellow flâneur Alfred Delvau, is somewhat misleading, since only a small portion of the book concerns "unknown Paris," being primarily a collection of Privat's letters, articles, short stories, poetry, and even a one-act vaudeville play.

In a key passage from *Unknown Paris*, Privat classifies the ragpickers who wander the city into three types: the déclassé drunk who, Privat implies, gives the "profession" a bad name; the modern street-savage, who survives more by chance than by wit; and, finally, "le chiffonnier artiste"—"the ragpicker artist, the bohemian, the philosopher, the man who once was something and whom misfortune sometimes, misconduct almost always, compels to fall again and again into the lowest depths of society." Privat's first book offers the reader many insights into these artists of the street, denizens of a Parisian subculture that could hardly have been widely known at the time and is only known today thanks mainly to Privat. *Paris Anecdote* is subtitled *Les industries inconnues* (Unknown Industries) and describes the strange *métiers* or professions that the urban underclass of the great city pursue.

Among the *métiers* Privat describes are "meat leasers" (*les loueurs de viande*): butchers who rent out prime quarters of beef, mutton, and veal for a small fee to owners of modest soup shops. The soup vendors then hang the prime cuts in their windows so customers will think the fare is made from the best meat when in reality it is made from offal. Another surprising profession is the one followed by Monsieur Salin, a "maggot maker" (*fabricant d'asticots*) who collects dead dogs and lets the carcasses rot in an attic so he can harvest maggots from the carrion, which he then sells to fishermen to use as bait. One of the more elaborate *métiers* is practiced by a man who calls himself Matagatos, a jovial bon vivant who came to Paris from the Pyrenees and fell in love with the city. As his obviously invented name indicates (*matas* "kill" + *gatos* "cats"), the man found his calling as a cat killer.

Matagatos roams the moonlit streets of Paris hunting cats while pretending to be a *chiffonnier*, "but only to give himself a social position." He is accompanied on his nighttime rounds through the alleys of Paris by two well-trained English terriers, one named Ralph, the other Sobrono, which Privat calls Matagatos's "suppliers." The Spaniard sells the cat pelts to furriers, who are doing well, thanks to "muff madness" (*manchonomanie*) among fashionable Parisians. The meat he sells to restauranteurs, who use it to make *gibelotte*, or fricassee of "rabbit." In his more respectable role as ragpicker, Matagatos has an arrangement with all the cooks in his quarter of Paris to take the skins of the animals they butcher so long as the skins are accompanied by the heads. In this way he collects enough rabbit heads to convince skeptical customers that the meat in their *gibelotte* is indeed rabbit.

Privat had a reputation as a *blagueur*, or joker, so every métier he describes may not have been practiced in fact. Was there really a woman whose métier was breeding ants for profit? And what about Mademoiselle Rose, who is supposed to have rented out leeches for medicinal purposes again and again, having figured out a way of making the creatures disgorge the blood of one client before cleaning and preparing them for the next patient? Still, no one had so much of what we now call "street cred" as Privat, who renders the *chiffoniers* and other members of the urban underclass so richly that we tend to believe such people must have really existed.

In *Paris Anecdote*, Privat uses the term *bohémien* only once—to describe someone from Valachie (Wallachia, the old name for Romania), whom he also calls "un Gypsy," that is, an ethnic Rom. But he also uses the term *artiste* to describe the eccentric practitioners of the unknown industries of Paris he details, as when he says of Monsieur Salin, the maggot maker, that he is "too artistic" to own property. Indeed, Privat understands all of the odd characters in *Paris Anecdote* as "artists" in a special sense: "To be an artist here means throwing money out the window, spending it indiscriminately,... drinking here and there,... singing, always laughing." At the same time, all these ragpickers and maggot makers are self-sufficient and do not have the need of any form of public welfare, a point Privat makes again and again, as when he observes that seeking help from the office of public assistance is "a disgrace for any man in these working-class neighborhoods."

The people who populate *Paris Anecdote* clearly belong to the same mongrel class that Marx called "bohemian" in *The Eighteenth Brumaire*, and it is easy to understand the basis for the disdain in which Marx held them: they may be working class, but they do not belong to that class of workers Marx sought to organize and incite to revolution. The "artists" Privat describes are too independent and individualistic ever to be organized into any form of collective political action. Indeed, their attitude toward public assistance shows that they were averse to the kind of state socialism Marx advocated.

While bohemians may not adhere to a consistent ideology across cultures, the combination of individualism and anti-statism—or, at least, a tendency to regard the neighborhood as a more meaningful political unit than the nation—brought many bohemians in Paris very close to anarchism. This is another ideological nuance that places one species of bohemian at a considerable ideological remove from Marxism, since nineteenth-century anarchists rejected the kind of communism Marx promoted as insufficiently accommodating to the rights and needs of individuals. For a while, Marx tried to unify the different ideological strains within the International Working Men's Association, founded in 1864, into a single revolutionary agenda, but in 1876 the so-called First International came to an end, mainly because of conflicts between the gradualist Marx and Mikhail Bakunin, the leader of those anarchists who advocated more immediate "direct action," a code name for violence.

Anarchism in the popular imagination is often misunderstood as anarchy, that is, chaos or disorder, and while it is true that Bakunin advocated violent revolution, the ideology could also be expressed through more rational and peaceful means so long as the basic freedoms of the individual were upheld against the authority of the state, and even the state was sometimes allowed so long as it served a purely administrative function. The most widespread theoretical model of this rational, peaceful variant of anarchism was provided by another of Marx's rivals, the political philosopher Pierre-Joseph Proudhon, who first used the term *anarchie* in a positive sense in 1851.

Proudhon's great political idea was to replace the system of legal restraints on individuals in society with a system of contractual obligations between and among free individuals or groups of individuals. For example, a cobbler could enter into a contract with a farmer to provide shoes for the farmer's family in exchange for food, or a group of farmers could form themselves into an autonomous collective that might form a contractual agreement with another collective—of carpenters, say—in order to obtain needed products and services. This form of anarchism is called *mutualist* because the system exists for the mutual benefit of all members of society equally. At the same time, the concept of political autonomy can be used to justify refusal to participate in society altogether, a form of anarchism often called *individualist*. Either way, it is easy to see how both the mutualist and the individualist models of anarchism harmonize with bohemian culture.

For most of the nineteenth century, actual examples of anarchist societies were few and far between. That changed on March 18, 1871, when the municipality of Paris—the *commune de Paris*—seceded from the nation of France and formed a government along anarchist lines in the chaotic aftermath of the demise of the Second Empire with the French defeat in the Franco-Prussian War of 1870–71. Although it lasted only about two months—ending on May 28, 1871, when the ragtag army of Communards were ruthlessly slaughtered by order of Adolph Thiers, the first president of the Third Republic (1870–1940)—the Paris Commune became the stuff of anarchist lore well into the twentieth century. Marx provided one of the best contemporary accounts of the Commune in another one of his pamphlets, *The Civil War in France* (1871), in which he interpreted the insurrection as the first example in history of "the dictatorship of the proletariat."

That it may have been, but the workers involved in the Commune tended to identify more with the anarchist philosophy of Proudhon than with the communist politics of Marx. In fact, when the first communal government was formed on March 28, 1871, twenty of Proudhon's followers were among the sixty-four elected members while only two supported Marx. Moreover, about half of that group of sixty-four belonged to the anarchist-friendly class of small tradesmen and artisans, while none were the factory workers that Marx courted as prospective revolutionaries. So the Communards were hardly Marxist and mostly anarchist, but conservative journalists called them something else—"bohemians," prompting the cultural historian Jerrold Siegel to reach the startling conclusion that "the origins and character of the Commune owed something to Bohemia." Indeed, it is hard to argue against the basic observation that anarchists, Communards, and bohemians are all cut from the same social cloth.

Understandably, the bohemian identification of those involved in the political struggles during the spring of 1871 in Paris goes against the grain of Marx's analysis of the social makeup of the

Communards. In fact, Marx invoked Bohemia in his condemnation of those who *opposed* the Communards. In *The Civil War in France*, he repeated the odd association of bohemianism and Bonapartism that he had made in *The Eighteenth Brumaire*, describing "the exodus from Paris of the high Bonapartist and capitalist bohème."

The addition of "capitalism" as an attribute of Marx's imagined Bohemia is something new, a connection he repeats further in the pamphlet when he describes "the Paris of M. Thiers" as a false, "phantom" Paris—"the Paris of the Boulevards, male and female—the rich, the capitalist, the gilded, the idle Paris, now thronging with its lackeys, its blacklegs, its literary *bohême*, and its *cocottes*." In a way, Marx the leftist supporter of the Communards who called their enemies "bohemians" and the conservative journalists who called those same Communards "bohemians" are both right, since two species of bohemian had long existed: even Murger distinguished between the authentic, impoverished type and the false, fashionable version. What is new is the emergence of bohemians as a political class, despite the uncertainty about the precise ideology bohemians embodied.

The difficulty of identifying "bohemian ideology" in a precise or consistent way notwithstanding, the late nineteenth-century alignment with anarchism combined with the long association of artists with bohemians has some far-reaching implications. Now, bohemian artists could also be considered revolutionary, not because of their political involvement, but because of their avant-garde art. The military metaphor "avant-garde" was adopted in the 1820s to describe the relationship of artists to society at large, the assumption being that artists had sensitivities that set them apart from ordinary mortals and allowed them to see beyond the present: the avant-garde artist might not have been appreciated in his own time but would be in the future. The philosopher Claude-Henri de Saint-Simon, who originated the metaphor comparing artistic vision to military reconnaissance, said that "things should move ahead with the artists in the lead, followed by the scientists, and that the industrialists should come after these two classes."

One such avant-garde artist was Gustave Courbet, whose realistic depictions of working-class life endeared him to anarchists, notably Proudhon. Indeed, Courbet played an important role in the Commune (though as an administrator, not an artist). Even though the idea of the avant-garde had been around for a long time, the overheated politics of the Commune intensified the sense of art as a revolutionary activity. In addition, the urban geography of Paris was favorable to the informal alliance of revolutionary politics, avant-garde art, and bohemian lifestyle because the one sector of the city that remained mostly untouched by Haussmann's modernization was Montmartre, especially the southern slope of the Butte.

The largely rural neighborhood was home to bohemians, anarchists, and artists alike, and of course those three identities were often represented in a single person, such as the young Pablo Picasso. Some of Murger's fictional bohemians, we recall, lived in "the Breda district," near Montmartre, a detail that reflects the historical reality that bohemian occupancy of the Butte did not have to wait until the 1870s. The importance of Montmartre to revolutionary history was certified at the very beginning of the Commune when forces loyal to the provisional government led by Thiers were defeated there by National Guardsmen loyal to the *commune de Paris* in March of 1871. In other words, the Commune was born on the slopes of Montmartre.

Estimates vary as to how many fighters loyal to the Commune were slaughtered in the aftermath of its collapse: the low-end estimate is six thousand dead, the high end thirty thousand, but historians today think ten thousand might be nearer the mark. Not all of those who died (whatever the number), either by

7. The Butte of Montmartre in the 1880s was little more than a scruffy landscape, or *maquis*, of shacks and old windmills.

defending the Commune or by summary execution afterward, were anarchists. But many were—enough, at any rate, to make the Commune legendary in the annals of anarchism. Montmartre got its name when early Christians called the hill "Mons Martyrum" to memorialize those who had sacrificed their lives for the faith, so the name fit with a new generation of political martyrs who had sacrificed their lives for the Commune.

That history played a role in the spread of anarchism into the bohemian bars and cafés of Montmartre in the 1880s and 1890s. In the late 1880s, several cafés and cabarets opened in some of the old windmills that dotted the top of the Butte. Miners, farmers, and other workers congregated in these converted windmills, drawn to the inexpensive food and cheap wine (the latter exempt from the excise tax café owners had to pay elsewhere in Paris). Among these establishments were the Moulin de la Galette, the Cabaret des Assassins, the Lapin Agile, and the Chat Noir, which also published a magazine with the same name. The Chat Noir is reputed to have had as its motto a saying attributed to the poet Charles Cros: "Wine is a red liquid, except in the morning, when it is white." Such acclaimed poets as Paul Verlaine drank absinthe and read their work in the cabaret, whose walls were decorated with paintings and sketches by the many artists drawn to Montmartre.

Another celebrated establishment was the Concert Lisbonne in lower Montmartre, run by Maxime Lisbonne, who had been arrested for serving as a colonel in the Communard forces (he was released from prison in 1880). His Communard background aroused government suspicion that the café was a "centre anarchiste," as a police report of April 30, 1894, explains:

> The Concert Lisbonne has always been a socialist-anarchist center. And Lisbonne, while being prudent, preciously tries to conserve his Communard title. His political past is very much in his present fortune, and it is not rare to hear a spectator say: he has been in the Commune, he has been a colonel, he has been deported, etc. The same political past assures him a politico-literary clientele.... He is entirely devoted to the literary anarchists, and he receives them privately in his secretarial office....

The report also numbers students, painters, and sculptors among Lisbonne's clientele; the café, in short, was precisely the kind of place that allowed Bohemia to flourish in Montmartre, which provided a cultural infrastructure based on the fortuitous combination of urban geography, radical politics, and avant-garde aesthetics.

This tripartite pattern emerged as a kind of template for bohemian culture, with late nineteenth-century Montmartre as the paradigm of that pattern. Indeed, Montmartre continued to nurture the development of modern art, at least until the outbreak of World War I in 1914. But in the early years of the twentieth century, Montmartre was not the only Montmartre: the bohemian mixture of politics, poverty, and art could be "exported" to other nations and neighborhoods, such as Greenwich Village in New York City. Montmartre was not even the only Montmartre in Paris, since the place could also be replicated in false form as an inauthentic copy of itself.

An early historian of the Butte observed that even as the "genuine Montmartre" somehow managed to continue, albeit in attenuated form, the "false Montmartre" gained momentum with the tourist industry. Montmartre, in short, was both "Athens and Babel," the latter identity evident especially at midnight, when "you will hear every language under the sun except French": "Side shows and fantastic spectacles are the attractions for those who come to this district where art is commercialized." From the beginning, Bohemia had a dual existence—or, at least, dual possibilities—as either a cultural sensibility or a business model (recall the success of Murger and Barrière's melodrama), but from the days of the false Montmartre onward the cultural and the commercial versions of Bohemia often coexisted.

"Montmartre in Manhattan" was the phrase once used to identify the Greenwich Village neighborhood as a bohemian enclave within New York City. So were "Gotham's Latin Quarter" and "America's Left Bank." The first of these three epithets is especially apt: as was Montmartre to Paris, so was Greenwich Village to New York. As its name suggests, the warren of streets lined with townhouses and tenements on Manhattan's lower west side seemed to be a village apart from the surrounding city. Originally inhabited by residents of colonial New York seeking a rural retreat from the bustling commercial sector of lower Manhattan (where the Wall Street financial district is today), the Village was not subjected to the strict north-south, east-west grid of streets urban planners imposed on most of the city. Instead, the streets and lanes followed the wandering paths of stream beds and old trails where sheep and cattle were once driven to market, crisscrossing one another at oblique, odd angles.

Even today, for example, one might meet a friend at the corner of Waverly Place and Waverly Place, where the east-west line of the street suddenly veers north. The eccentric street plan truly gives the Village a different feel from other, more geometrically regular New York neighborhoods. Floyd Dell, one of the most important of the pre-war bohemians in the Village, worried in 1916 that the southward extension of Seventh Avenue (which stopped at 12th Street), combined with new subway stations, would make it easier for "barbarians from Uptown" to infiltrate the area and bring their

8. The urban plan of Greenwich Village shows the contrast of its crooked streets with the strict grid of adjacent Manhattan neighborhoods.

conformity with them: "The crooked streets will be straightened out. The old houses with their high ceilings and fireplaces will be torn down. The section will become simply a part of New York."

Fortunately, the extension now known as Seventh Avenue South did not alter the urban geography of the Village as dramatically as Dell feared (the crooked streets still exist, as well as the old houses with high ceilings). Prior to World War I, the Village was the bohemian home to any number of anarchists and socialists who found common cause in their opposition to capitalism despite their differing ideologies. Dell was a key member of a radical institution known as the Liberal Club, formerly located slightly uptown at Gramercy Park. In 1912, the club moved to 137 MacDougal Street, just off Sixth Avenue, where it served as both an arts center and a political center until 1918.

The ideological orientation of the club was socialist at a time when socialism was at its apogee in the United States. In the basement of the club, however, an anarchist from Evanston, Illinois, named Paula Holladay ran a working-class eatery that the locals called Polly's Restaurant even though it had no formal name. Dell says that the combination of the Liberal Club and Polly's Restaurant provided something that "had never been in the Village before, a common meeting place." The cook and waiter at Polly's was Hippolyte Havel, another anarchist (and ex-lover of the anarchist Emma Goldman) who was known to denounce the members of the Liberal Club when he served them as "bourgeois pigs!"

Many members of the club also worked—for free—as editors and writers for *The Masses*, the socialist magazine founded in 1911 by Piet Vlag, a Dutch immigrant and restaurant manager, who served as editor-in-chief until that post was assumed by Max Eastman in late 1912. Eastman was in graduate school at Columbia University studying philosophy with John Dewey when he received a letter from a group of writers and artists associated with the magazine informing him, out of the blue, "You are elected editor of *The Masses*. No pay." One of Eastman's first acts was to collaborate with John Reed, later celebrated for his first-hand account of the Russian Revolution, *Ten Days That Shook the World* (1919), on a manifesto that would appear on the inside front cover of the magazine for the duration of its publication thereafter:

> This Magazine is Owned and Published Co-operatively by Its Editors. It has no Dividends to Pay, and nobody is trying to make Money out of it. A Revolutionary and not a Reform Magazine; a Magazine with a Sense of Humor and no Respect for the Respectable; Frank; Arrogant; Impertinent; searching for the True Causes; a Magazine directed against Rigidity and Dogma wherever it is found; Printing what is too Naked or True for a Money-making Press; a Magazine whose final Policy is to do as it Pleases and Conciliate Nobody, not even its Readers—There is a Field for this Publication in America. Help us to find it.

The manifesto captures the ideological intensity not only of *The Masses*, but also of the bohemian community in Greenwich Village more generally. Indeed, it is not too much to say that the Village during the pre-war era was home to the most radical bohemian community, before or since, in the United States.

A specific example of the exceptional politics of Greenwich Village concerns the role of women in its bohemian circles just before World War I. Most prior bohemian cultures relegated women to the traditional roles of muse, model, or mistress. There are exceptions to this general pattern, such as Fanny zu Reventlow in Schwabing, but for the most part meaningful, equal involvement in bohemian culture lay outside the domain of women. That pattern changed in Greenwich Village. In his autobiography, Dell describes any number of women whose contributions to the radical community of Village bohemians were indispensable to the wider success of that community. Paula Holladay not only provided a common meeting place for artists and writers but also used her restaurant to help feed the poor. A high school teacher named Henrietta Rodman extended the reach of the Liberal Club to students at nearby New York University and to the several settlement houses in downtown New York (notably the Henry Street Settlement on the Lower East Side) that catered to the needs of the immigrant poor.

Historically, the most important woman associated with the socialist Bohemia of Greenwich Village was the birth control advocate Margaret Sanger, who in 1914 began publication of her own radical magazine, *The Woman Rebel* (the slogan underneath the title read, "No Gods, No Masters"). The larger purpose of the publication, announced in the first issue of March 1914, was "to stimulate working women to think for themselves and to build up a conscious fighting character." Its more specific aim was "to advocate for the prevention of conception and to impart such knowledge in the columns of this paper," as well as to expose the injustice resulting from police persecution of the roughly 35,000 women working as prostitutes in New York City.

Sanger did not present her advocacy for working-class women as a feminist program because she harbored considerable skepticism about American feminism, which she found too middle class, merely a "weak echo" of the English campaign for suffrage. Although Sanger is usually identified as a socialist, the most telling ideological moment in the initial manifesto of *The Woman Rebel* comes when Sanger challenges feminists to abandon respectability and other presumed female virtues so they can assert themselves more forcefully: "How many of you could be a Voltairine de Clayre [*sic*], a Louise Michel, an Emma Goldman, or an Elizabeth Flynn?" Apart from Flynn, a socialist who did advocate for a woman's right to vote, these women were anarchists for whom female suffrage was mostly beside the larger revolutionary point.

Sanger's dismissive attitude toward contemporary feminists was countered by Crystal Eastman, Max's sister, who understood the cause of contraception as only one element of a broader program of social reform. Like her better-known brother, Crystal Eastman advocated revolutionary socialism but recognized that the economic freedom women needed could not wait for the revolution. Rather, as she wrote in 1918, women were due "such economic freedom as it is possible for a human being to achieve under the existing system of competitive production and distribution,—in short such freedom to choose one's way of making a living as men now enjoy." She argued that "the economic is the fundamental aspect of feminism" and insisted that "Birth Control"—the term Sanger invented in 1914—"is an elementary essential in all aspects of feminism." Sanger's doubts about middle-class suffragists were hardly shared by Eastman, an active and instrumental advocate for a woman's right to vote, but she too was impatient with her fellow feminists' single-minded focus on the issue. Writing in Sanger's *Birth Control Review*, Eastman maintained that "the whole structure of the feminist's dream of society rests upon the rapid extension of scientific knowledge about birth control," adding: "This seems so obvious to me that I was astonished the other day to come upon a group of distinguished feminists who discussed for an hour what could be done with the woman's vote in New York State and did not once mention birth control."

Both Sanger and Eastman did everything they could to provide the information women needed to take sexual responsibility for their own lives. That information ran afoul of the same obscenity laws devised to prevent the transmission of pornography and other illicit materials through the U.S. mail, a moralistic cause led by the purity campaigner Anthony Comstock. Comstock was not a government agent but the president of the New York Society for the Suppression of Vice, a private organization founded in 1873. The society exercised considerable influence on municipal and federal officials to assure "the enforcement of laws for the suppression of the trade in, and circulation of obscene literature and illustrations, advertisements, and articles of indecent or immoral use." The information about birth control that Sanger tried to provide to working-class women fell under Comstock's definition of obscenity and indecency.

Dell gives an account of female readers' responses to a series of articles about Sanger in *The Masses*, explaining how the magazine received "thousands of letters" requesting information about birth control which Dell was legally prohibited from providing. In his public editorial role, Dell dutifully informed the women of the legal restraints against him, but then, he explains, "as a private individual, I carefully turned over all these letters to other private individuals, who mailed this information to the women." For her part, Sanger was indicted under the Comstock laws for publishing *The Woman Rebel* and *Family Limitation*, a brief illustrated manual of birth control methods also issued in 1914. To avoid what she thought was almost certain conviction, Sanger left the United States for wartime England, traveling under an assumed name. On her return, her case garnered widespread public support and was eventually dismissed.

The illegal maneuvers Dell took to actively support Sanger's birth control movement were matched by the publicity accorded Sanger in the progressive pages of *The Masses*, consistent with the radical tenor of the magazine. One might expect an equal emphasis on the injustices suffered by African Americans in an era when racial segregation had been institutionalized at the federal level by the administration of President Woodrow Wilson. But the Black worker did not figure into the concerns of *The Masses* in the same way that the woman worker did, nor were Black people involved in the Greenwich Village Bohemia. That changed with the arrival of the Jamaican-born poet Claude McKay, who had been working as a Pullman porter before Crystal Eastman invited him to the offices of *The Liberator*, the new magazine she and her brother started up in 1918.

The Masses had been shut down after its antiwar editors were indicted "for conspiracy to obstruct the operations of the military laws of the country." To avoid a like fate, the Eastman siblings adopted a more moderate tone for the new magazine, despite the shift in ideological emphasis from mostly homegrown socialism to active support of Russian communism, especially after the founding of the Soviet Union in 1922 (*The Liberator* continued publication until 1924). The editorial offices of *The Liberator* were on Union Square East, just out of the proper confines of Greenwich Village but still downtown and still at a radical address. In the Village proper, Bohemia continued apace, especially after Prohibition took effect in January 1920, having been passed into law in a year earlier.

McKay published his best-known poem, "If We Must Die," in the July 1919 issue of *The Liberator*:

If we must die—let it not be like hogs
Hunted and penned in an inglorious spot,
While round us bark the mad and hungry dogs,
Making their mock at our accursed lot.
If we must die—oh, let us nobly die,
So that our precious blood may not be shed
In vain; then even the monsters we defy
Shall be constrained to honor us though dead!
O kinsmen! We must meet the common foe;
Though far outnumbered, let us still be brave,
And for their thousand blows deal one death-blow!
What though before us lies the open grave?
Like men we'll face the murderous, cowardly pack,
Pressed to the wall, dying, but—fighting back!

The poem was written in response to retaliations against Black people after allegations of Bolshevik involvement in race riots during the "Red Scare" summer of 1919. Despite newspaper headlines screaming "REDS TRY TO STIR NEGROES TO REVOLT," the radical left played a relatively small role in incitement to the protests that led to mob violence, with Blacks and whites fighting one another in the streets. More important factors included inadequate housing for Black people as well as competition for jobs as ever greater numbers of African Americans migrated north during the Jim Crow Era.

In later years, "If We Must Die" began to be read as a "universal" paean to heroic resistance against impossible odds, but McKay clearly had something more particular in mind, as other poems in *The Liberator* show. One addresses "the barrier of race" to a Black man's love for a white woman, while another captures the horror of lynching in appropriately violent terms:

> Black Southern men, like hogs await your doom!
> White wretches hunt and haul you from your huts,
> They squeeze the babies out your women's womb,
> They cut your members off, rip out your guts!

Whatever its universalist implications, in its original publication context "If We Must Die" specifically refers not only to the racially motivated killings of Black people in the 1919 race riots but also to a larger history of violent racism.

McKay's association with *The Liberator* became more formal in 1921 when he became a coeditor, but he resigned in 1922 amid disagreements with the Eastmans over editorial policy, as he became increasingly disappointed by the American left's failures to adequately confront racism. Unfortunately, the stereotype of Black people as culturally more "primitive" or "vital" than whites was especially widespread in the 1920s, a stereotype that continued to be cultivated among otherwise enlightened left-leaning bohemians in Greenwich Village. Even Max Eastman was not wholly immune to this stereotype, writing in his introduction to McKay's *Harlem Shadows* (1922) that the poems are representative of "that most alien race among us" and "characteristic of that race as we most admire it—they are gentle-simple, candid, brave, and friendly, quick of laughter and of tears." In his introduction Eastman did acknowledge the problem of racial prejudice, but his comments about what he perceived as the "quality of simple-heartedness" in McKay's poetry reveals his own unconscious bias, however "positive."

Some African Americans embraced the stereotype of the simple-hearted Black primitive Eastman described and knowingly exploited it, the best example being Josephine Baker, who in the 1920s danced practically nude before mostly white audiences in Paris nightclubs, wearing only a short skirt festooned with "bananas" fashioned out of stuffed fabric. McKay's disillusionment with the leftist bohemians of Greenwich Village who failed to confront racism and Baker's exhibitionistic exploitation of "primitive" Blackness both argue, perhaps in different ways, for the discomforting fact that Black experience figured in bohemian culture primarily as something that whites could claim as validation of their own social status as "bohemian." This dynamic seems to have been quite pervasive in Jazz Age New York, when the clubs and speakeasies in the Black neighborhood of Harlem became the cultural destination of choice for white elites seeking "authentic" bohemian experiences.

Those types of experiences were captured in a novel by Carl Van Vechten that suggests how far removed from political radicalism bohemian culture had become in New York City by 1930, when the novel was published. The title *Parties: Scenes from Contemporary New York Life* includes an allusion to Murger's *Scenes of Bohemian Life*, but the bohemians in the novel are nothing like either the hapless characters Murger chronicled or the leftist figures that populated Greenwich Village a decade or so before the time of Van Vechten's novel. His characters are all well-to-do white New Yorkers and decadent European aristocrats whose life is an endless round of parties at jazz clubs and speakeasies—most of them in Harlem—and who "might be described as cosmopolitan," although "bohemian—if one may revive a worn out epithet that once meant a great deal—would be a more exact word."

Floyd Dell became aware early on that bohemian radicalism could easily degenerate into bohemian hedonism of the sort that Van Vechten describes in *Parties*, warning that politics and alcohol do not mix. Perhaps with Marx's well-known comparison of religion to a drug—"the opiate of the masses"—Dell compares alcohol to Christianity because both help "to endure the temporal ills of the flesh." But where Christianity only offers paradise as a future reward, a good stiff drink actually provides it in the here and now: "an existence, for the moment, free from responsibility." What Dell describes as inimical to the political Bohemia he knew is part of the internal dynamic of all Bohemias, whose adherents take their pleasures wherever they find them without caring about tomorrow. No doubt government oppression of radical politics and the hard rightward shift in U.S. immigration policies played a role in the demise of Greenwich Village's political Bohemia, but Dell is right to say that the social revolution depends more on collective action than the sort of individual satisfaction the bohemian hedonist pursues. The political bohemians of Greenwich Village may have wanted to make art for life's sake, but in the end life got in the way of the revolution they wanted their art to advocate.

Chapter 4
Artistic Bohemias

Through all its fictional, historical, and political permutations, Bohemia has had its share of visual artists. Eugene Delacroix painted the young George Sand in male garb when she was writing novels about vagabond bohemians devoted to their art, and the artist Camille Corot decorated the rooms of the bohemians who congregated at the Impasse du Doyenné. In the mid-nineteenth century, notable artists such as Gustave Courbet and James McNeill Whistler began to call themselves "bohemians" as a way of capturing their artistic positioning relative to society at large. The development marks a change—two changes, really— from earlier manifestations of bohemian culture: first, prior bohemians were mostly writers, not visual artists (with some exceptions); and second, bohemian identity was usually provisional, not permanent—a stage, not a state. Increasingly, bohemian artists who experienced a period of impoverishment maintained the bohemian identity once they achieved success, the economic condition having been subsumed by the cultural condition.

Even today, the sociology of the contemporary art world forms along the lines of mainstreams and margins, cultures and countercultures, insiders and outsiders—all very much a part of the bohemian heritage. Such positioning, begun in the era of Courbet's realism and Whistler's impressionism, continued into various twentieth-century avant-gardes, whether in Zurich, Madrid, Buenos Aires, Managua, Rome, or some other metropolis. However key those cities may have been in providing the urban conditions conducive to artistic Bohemia, none can compare to Paris. Indeed, the history of modern art is all but inseparable from the urban history of two bohemian neighborhoods in the City of Light: first Montmartre, then Montparnasse.

As for Courbet, he associated himself with several bohemian groups over his life, including the one that formed around Henry Murger at the Café Momus in the 1840s as well as another group that met at the Brasserie des Martyrs, a Right Bank café managed by a gentleman with the unlikely last name of Bourgeois. Murger and his friends also frequented the Brasserie, along with that arch-bohemian, Alexandre Privat d'Anglemont. So the artist was very much a part of the urban scene of Paris Bohemia, which had a meaning for Courbet that seems to have been quite new.

Whereas Murger, for example, saw Bohemia as a stage of artistic development on the way to professional success, Courbet did not really leave Bohemia behind once he became successful. On the contrary, however much he may have won over the official art establishment with his work, he continued to cultivate an outsider, bohemian identity because—and this is key—he understood how interrelated the margins and the mainstream really were, to the point where being outside the official art establishment all but guaranteed ultimate acceptance by it. Hence Courbet's importance for art history lies not only in the revolutionary style he called realism but also in the way he navigated the changing social circumstances of the profession of artist. After Courbet, rejection by the establishment both validated the worth of the independent artist and assured even greater success in the future—so long as the artist maintained the identity of "bohemian," that is, a rebel, an outsider, an independent, an individualist.

Given the important role of the state in nineteenth-century France in certifying and sustaining the careers of acceptable artists— those whose work could only be exhibited if officially sanctioned by the salon—it is understandable that Courbet would be drawn to both anarchism and Bohemia, the first because it rejected the state outright, the second because it provided an alternative artistic community with no state affiliation. Courbet came to Paris from the farming village of Ornans and made no effort to hide his rural origins; in fact, Courbet's countrified manners were very much a part of his bohemian identity, not to mention the countryside itself, to which the artist returned whenever he felt the need to shore up his outsider status. In 1850 he wrote to a friend, "Even in our civilized society, I must live the life of a savage. I must break free from its very governments....Therefore I have just embarked on the great wandering and independent life of the bohemian." Courbet did not have it both ways so much as he had each way halfway: as the son of a wealthy landowner, by one reckoning Courbet was bourgeois to the core. By another reckoning he was something of a peasant, who spoke in the rural patois of the province where he was born. Put peasant and bourgeois together in roughly equal measures and what you get is a bohemian.

Courbet died in 1877, right around the time that Montmartre began to emerge more fully as both a political and an artistic Bohemia. But the bourgeois peasant from Ornans would surely have felt at home on the Butte, where people still raised chickens and goats. Émile Zola describes the rural landscape of Montmartre in *L'assommoir* (1877), a novel about hard-drinking working-class types (the title means, literally, "a blow to the head" and refers to alcoholic blackouts) that focuses on a poor washerwoman named Gervais. Walking along a muddy roadway, Gervais comes upon stretch of waste land: "Lying between a sawmill and a button factory, this last remaining strip of green had yellow patches where the grass was scorched; a goat, tethered to a stake, was bleating as it circled round and round, while on the far side a dead tree rotted away in the sunshine." Gervaise takes in the scene and remarks, "Just look!"... "You'd think you were in the country!"

The Butte of Montmartre remained pretty much as Zola described it—and as Vincent Van Gogh, Jean-François Raffaelï, and others painted it—even after the *funiculaire* was built in 1902, making access to the top of the hill easier. As part of the newly formed eighteenth arrondissement, it really did seem like a small country village apart from the metropolis. We know from Murger and other sources that Montmartre had been home to bohemians even before the Haussmann modernization priced them out of other neighborhoods in Paris, but once that modernization began the area offered natural geographical resistance to it: at an elevation of some 428 feet the Butte posed a challenge to the radiating, horizontal plan of the urban transformation. Montmartre retained its rural, village-like atmosphere in the face of modernization, preserving the look and feel of a much earlier era. Indeed, the idea of Montmartre as a village apart from Paris proper continued for some time, as the title of a 1939 film about the neighborhood shows—*Un village dans Paris* (A village within Paris, dir. Pierre Harts). To this day, the official website of the Paris tourist bureau calls the area an "authentic village in the heart of Paris."

Montmartre was a tourist Bohemia long before the Convention and Visitors Bureau of Paris promoted it as such. That Bohemia, however, was located mainly at the Moulin Rouge and other nightspots near the base of the Butte, where the *chansonnier* Aristide Bruant sang songs derived from the argot spoken by the petty criminals at the top of the Butte. Bruant is an important figure in the history of Montmartre's artistic Bohemia for several reasons, including his own contributions in the form of popular music. He was also responsible for assuring the continuing survival of one of the most significant bohemian venues in the history of modern art: the Lapin Agile, a cabaret at the top of

Montmartre that served as a second home to the young Pablo Picasso and numerous other artists at the outset of their careers.

The place was slated for destruction in 1902 when Bruant bought it, leasing it shortly thereafter to Fréderick Gérard, known as Frédé. Picasso painted the bearded, guitar-playing bohemian wearing his peasant clogs in the shallow background of *Au Lapin Agile* (ca. 1904–5), featuring a self-portrait of himself garbed as Harlequin clutching a glass of absinthe at the bar beside a female companion. The cabaret had formerly been known as the Cabaret des Assassins, after the portraits of murderers painted on the walls. In 1875 the caricaturist André Gill painted a sign showing an agile rabbit wearing a cap, bow tie, and cummerbund stepping out of a saucepan, balancing a bottle of wine on its right foreleg. At some point, the locals started calling the Cabaret des Assassins the Lapin Agile, the name being a double pun: *Lapin à Gill* (Rabbit by Gill) or *Là peint A. Gill* (There painted A. Gill). When Frédé took over, he made the informal name official and painted over the legend "Cabaret des Assassins" on the outside wall and replaced it with "Cabaret Artistique."

The Lapin Agile maintained its bohemian allure for more than a decade, at least until 1911, when Frédé's son, Victor, was shot to death at the cabaret, an event that seemed like a tragic, symbolic end to Montmartre as a center of modern art. Less symbolic was the start of the long-delayed development of the southern slope of the Butte in 1910, prompting many artists to move on to the more upscale but still bohemian neighborhood of Montparnasse. But in the first ten years or so of the twentieth century artists who would go on to be foundational figures of modernism were drawn to the neighborhood in unprecedented numbers. In addition to the Spaniard Picasso, *haut* Montmartre hosted Henri Matisse from northern France, Kees van Dongen from the Netherlands, Amedeo Modigliani from Italy, as well as the Paris natives Georges Braque, André Derain, Maurice de Vlaminck, and Maurice Utrillo, the only member of these modernists actually born in Montmartre.

Utrillo aside, then, one has to ask: What brought all these artists to this sketchy, backward neighborhood atop the hill overlooking the capital of modernity? So posed, the question contains its own answer, at least in part—namely, modernity. But living in Montmartre was not, paradoxically, quite the same as living in Paris. That was part of its bohemian appeal, given that one of the more consistent attributes of bohemians is their tendency not to be not fully a part of the city they are in.

Perhaps Montmartre, then, made it possible for artists to respond to modernity while not being entirely integrated into it, to stand apart from it and register its effects creatively in their work. At a less abstract level, the bohemian appeal of Montmartre was also—perhaps largely—economic. When these artists first came to the Butte they were impoverished: there are stories of Picasso painting while sitting on the floor because he could not afford a chair. And for a time he had to borrow shoes when he went out because he did not own a pair (in this Picasso was not unlike Murger, who at one point had to borrow trousers to leave his garret). Fortunately, the French franc had been remarkably stable for some time, such that one could buy a baguette or a bottle of wine in the early 1900s for the same price as in 1875.

And as for all those bars and cabarets where the artists gathered, the draw was not just interesting conversations and lively debates about art with other patrons, but credit: Frédé, for example, allowed the artists to run up a tab at the Lapin Agile and pay whatever they could whenever they could. Perhaps his generosity derived from his own training as an artist (he studied at the École d'Arts et Métiers in Gagny, a suburb of Paris) and the hardscrabble life he led prior to operating the Lapin Agile, when he worked as a fish-seller who also sold the odd painting out of his cart.

Frédé's early experience as a combination fishmonger and down-market art dealer points to another economic rationale for emerging artists to take up residence in Montmartre. Most of the bohemian hangouts like the Chat Noir, the Moulin de la Galette, and the Lapin Agile were also places where artists could display their work. The practice of young artists first presenting their work on the walls of cafés and restaurants continues to this day, but bohemian Montmartre may well have been where the practice began. The informal galleries at the top of the Butte served as an entry point to more legitimate galleries and drew the attention of early collectors. The lessening of the role of the state salon in the art market created the economic need for some other mechanism to both create and satisfy demand, and a loose confederation of gallerists, collectors, and picture vendors in Montmartre helped to meet that need.

Ambroise Vollard, the best known of these early gallerists, opened his first small shop at the base of the Butte in 1893, where he chose as his first exhibition several paintings from the studio of Édouard Manet, evidently originating the idea of the solo show. He also dealt in works by Pierre-August Renoir, Edgar Degas, and Paul Cezanne. Two years later he moved to a larger space near his original gallery and staged the first Paris exhibition of paintings by Vincent Van Gogh. In 1901 he exhibited a collection of new works by Picasso, which received a favorable review describing the art as a Spanish invasion, but a necessary one—an infusion of "barbarian" energy that might arrest the decline of France, no less. The formulation is a familiar one: contemporary culture has become senescent, decadent, and "feminine," so much so that it requires the spontaneity and virility Picasso allegedly embodies to recover from the sickness of excessive civilization. The notice was written by one Félicien Fagus, pen name of Georges-Eugène Faillet, an anarchist whose father had been a Communard. Surely the concord of artists and anarchists in the bohemian enclave of Montmartre did not hurt Picasso's chances of receiving such a sympathetic first review of his painting.

The anarchist context is only one example of how the earlier bohemian culture of Montmartre facilitated the development of modern art. Frédé could not possibly have known how completely he predicted that development when he changed the description of the Lapin Agile from "Cabaret des Assassins" to "Cabaret Artistique," but the through-line that runs from Montmartre to modernism could not be clearer. The painting Picasso did of himself at the bar of the Lapin Agile and that once hung on the walls of the cabaret itself now hangs in the Metropolitan Museum of Art in New York.

But the artistic legacy of Montmartre is hardly limited to modernism, having also left its mark on popular culture, even though that fugitive tradition is far less likely to receive the sort of official recognition museum exhibition entails. Perversely, the popular culture of Montmartre is known today almost entirely because of museum culture: the chanteuse Yvette Guilbert and the *chansonnier* Aristide Bruant are more familiar these days as figures in the poster art of Henri de Toulouse-Lautrec than as artists in their own right. Yet artists they were: if anything, their work registers the artistic Bohemia of Montmartre in much more vivid fashion than that of the post-impressionist and modernist painters who were their contemporaries. And no less than the painters, the singers provided the basis for a new artistic tradition—a street culture with roots in bohemian experience—that would continue deep into the twentieth century.

Yvette Guilbert's success—first in Paris, then internationally—would not have been possible without Bohemia. After several failed attempts singing the repertoire that was fashionable in the 1880s—songs popularized by "bellowing singers" (*chanteuses de beuglant*) who wore bouffant dresses—in 1892 Guilbert performed at the Chat Noir and began a professional relationship with the *chansonnier* Léon Xanrof, whose song collection *Chansons sans gêne* (Familiar songs) became a major part of her new repertoire. She also remade her stage persona around the same time, dispensing with the bouffant dress and adopting a long trailing gown that highlighted her gaunt, almost emaciated figure, accented with her trademark long black gloves, her face a white mask with a vivid gash of red lipstick.

One of her most popular Xanrof songs was "Le Fiacre" (a type of horse-drawn carriage), a jaunty tune that imitates the jogging of the horse: the words tell of a couple making love inside the carriage when a man on the street hears the woman's voice and realizes it belongs to his wife. Since adultery is almost the national pastime of France, the song seems more amusing than shocking.

Two ways of looking at Yvette Guilbert

There she is! A long leech, sexless. She crawls and creeps along, hissing as she goes, leaving behind a wavy trail of drool. With a funereal air she advances, undulating disdainfully, almost inert, like a worm. On each side of her boneless body hang, sadly tattered, tentacles gloved in mourning. She will certainly lead to the burial of our Latin race. She is the complete negation of our native genius...all that once rose joyfully up to the sky—she obscures, defiles, debases.

—Maurice Lefèvre, "Les gestes de la chanson," (1896)

The art of Yvette Guilbert is certainly the art of realism. She brings before you the real drama of the streets...she shows you the seamy side of life behind the scenes; she calls things by their right names. But there is not a touch of sensuality about her, she is neither contaminated nor contaminating by what she sings; she is simply a great, impersonal, dramatic artist, who sings realism as others write it.

—Arthur Symons, Colour Studies in Paris (1918)

Nonetheless, some critics heard in her music and saw in her stage presence the ruin of France, while others regarded Guilbert as a true artist in the tradition of naturalism, as two contrasting critical responses, the first by the Belgian poet Maurice Lefèvre, the second by the English poet Arthur Symons, illustrate.

Despite his own affiliation with the Chat Noir, Lefèvre preferred the *chanson populaire* to the more realistic *chanson moderne* that made up Guilbert's repertoire in the 1890s. As for Symons, he was much more attuned to the sense of decadence that Lefèvre decried, having recently written "The Decadent Movement in Literature" (1893) around the time he first heard Guilbert sing. However different their responses, both critics were responding to the very thing that made her a star: her ability to bring Bohemia to the bourgeoisie. As she wrote in her autobiography, she was "the first to bring the spirit ... of the Butte to the boulevards" and "propagate the verve of the Chat Noir" in venues like the Moulin Rouge and other cabarets that had a decidedly more bourgeois clientele than did the Chat Noir and the Lapin Agile.

Aristide Bruant, even more than Guilbert, remained faithful to Bohemia while still making a career of it. As one commentator wrote of him in 1925, the year he died, "Bruant contrived to become the idol of the lower classes whilst also holding a high place in the regard of the more cultured classes." He started at the Chat Noir, writing and performing his own songs. When the owner of that legendary cabaret decided to move to a more tourist-friendly arrondisement he took the name with him, whereupon Bruant rented out the place and renamed it Le Mirliton (The Reed-Pipe). There Bruant performed night after night, insulting his customers by calling them "pimps" and "scoundrels," which became part of the draw for tourists seeking the "authentic" bohemian experience.

Bruant also sang about pimps and scoundrels, taking the French chanson in a new direction that is now known as the *chanson realiste*, a further, grittier development of the *chansons modernes* that Guilbert helped to popularize. Many of these songs take their titles from the rougher neighborhoods and places of Paris: "A la Place Maubert" (in the Latin Quarter); "A la Villette," "A Saint-Ouen," "Belleville-Ménilmontant" (all suburbs of Paris); "A St. Lazarre," and "A la Roquette" (both prisons). "A Montpernesse" (the argot version of "A Montparnasse") is a song about an alcoholic prostitute married to her pimp, who murders her when he discovers she is sneaking out—not to be with another man, but to drink; the song ends with the pimp in prison, perfectly at peace with himself as he awaits the guillotine. In "Belleville-Ménilmontant," Bruant assumed the persona of a young criminal who pimps out his own little sister, "Cecille, in Belleville."

In his songs and other endeavors, Bruant adopted the cultural strategy pioneered by Courbet of making his bohemian identity a large part of his mainstream appeal. A one-man culture industry, Bruant published a journal keyed to his cabaret, *Le Mirliton*, which appeared off and on from 1885 to 1894; he also published several collections of his songs, a serial novel titled *Les bas-fonds de Paris* (The lower depths of Paris, 1897–1902), a weekly newspaper called *La lanterne de Bruant*, and a dictionary of Parisian street slang. By the first years of the twentieth century, Bruant had become so wealthy from his various endeavors that he mostly retired from singing. It was around this time that he bought the Lapin Agile to save it from demolition, adding that distinction to a resume that makes Bruant perhaps the most important bohemian celebrity since Murger.

Bruant's influence continued well into the twentieth century as the tradition of the *chanson réaliste* he originated was taken up by a new class of female singer who, unlike Guilbert and other nineteenth-century *chanteuses*, had lived the life of the bohemian street they sang about. One of the more acclaimed of these *chanteuse réalistes* was known professionally as Fréhel (born Marguerite Boulc'h), whose biography almost defies belief. Before World War I, she had scores of lovers, including the young Maurice Chevalier and the boxer Jack Johnson. When the war broke out, she was singing in Russia and was unable to return to France, so she went first to Bucharest, then Istanbul.

She became a drug addict and got to be enormously overweight by the time she returned to France in 1925, when she resumed her singing career under the name "Madame Sans-Gêne" (Mrs. Shameless). "J'ai l'cafard" (literally, "I have the cockroach" but idiomatically "I'm feeling blue"), a song from 1928, was written specifically for her so she could give voice to some of the sordid things she had experienced firsthand:

Dans ma névrose j'ai pris des tas d'choses	I'm depressed; I've taken tons of things,
Éther, morphine, et coco	Ether, morphine, and cocaine,
Drogues infâmes	Evil drugs
Qui charment les femmes	That lure women,
Pour mieux noyer leurs cerveaux	All the better to crush their brains,
En songeant que chaque goutte	Even as I know that every drop
De ce poison qui m'dégoûte	Of that disgusting poison
Mène mon corps	Drags my body
Vers la mort	To its death.

In the early 1930s, a French journalist called Fréhel "a misbegotten daughter of Aristide Bruant and Yvette Guilbert" as a way of describing the continuing cultural tradition all three singers represented. The journalist's trope might be extended by imagining that Fréhel also had a "misbegotten daughter" of the Paris streets herself: Édith Piaf, the most celebrated chanteuse of them all.

Born Édith Gassione and abandoned by her mother at birth, the child was shuffled about among her father's relatives until she was deposited at the age of five or six (accounts vary) in the town of Bernay in Normandy, at a *maison close*, or brothel, where her paternal grandmother worked as the house cook. After a year or two living in the brothel with her grandmother, she was introduced to the vagabond life when her father turned up and took his daughter on the road with him (he was a street performer who did acrobatic tricks for cash). By the time Édith arrived in Pigalle by way of Belleville on the outskirts of Paris, she had learned how to scrape together a living by singing on the street.

In 1933 she landed her first professional job at a lesbian nightclub on Rue Pigalle in Montmartre. The place was called Les Juan-de-Pins (after the resort town on the Riviera east of Cannes) but more familiarly known as Chez Lulu. The job helped Édith to realize that her powerful voice—always startling because of her petite frame (she stood two inches short of five feet)—might lead to a more stable career. Lucienne Franchi, the owner of the club whom everyone called Lulu, dressed Édith and her friend Simone Bertaut, with whom she performed, in sailor costumes, which the customers found appealing; sometimes Simone would shed her outfit and perform in the nude, which the customers found more appealing. The clientele of the club included pimps, prostitutes, and members of the *milieu*, as the French mafia is called, precisely the type of audience attuned to the hard-edged songs that make up the repertoire of the *chanteuses réalistes*.

There was one song that Lulu's customers wanted to hear Édith sing again and again: "Comme un moineau" (Like a sparrow)—a song that Fréhel had made popular. The song tells the story of a young woman who turns to prostitution to escape poverty, becoming inured to the hardships of streetlife as time goes by. In 1935, after she had left Lulu's, a nightclub owner heard Édith singing "Comme un moineau" on the street and asked her to audition for him at his club in a fashionable area of Paris near the

Champs-Elysées. The song also inspired the idea to change her last name (Gassion sounded too "common"), but another singer had already claimed "Moineau" so Édith settled on "Piaf," Parisian street slang for "sparrow," a better choice because her background as a bohemian street singer was as much a part of her appeal as her remarkable voice.

The *réaliste* world that Bruant, Fréhel, and Piaf sang about has clear roots in Bohemia and belongs to the urban subculture usually termed the "other Paris" or the "secret Paris," although by the 1920s the borders of bohemian society and bourgeois society had become so porous that the "other Paris" hardly appears "other" at all and the "secret" seems well out in the open. Such is the impression, anyway, created by the documentary photographs of bohemian haunts shot by the French-Romanian photographer Gyula Halász, known as Brassaï. In two of his books, *Paris de nuit* (*Paris by Night*, 1933) and *Le Paris secret des années 30* (*The Secret Paris of the '30s*, 1976), Brassaï's camera focuses on carnival barkers, fortune tellers, cesspool cleaners, petty criminals, and such eccentric individuals as "the queen of Montmartre's nocturnal fauna," the fantastically bejeweled older woman known as "La Môme Bijou" (the name is ironic because *la môme* means "kid" or "brat"). But Brassaï includes enough shots of the occasional bourgeois gentleman out on the town—or in the brothel—as to suggest that this "secret Paris" was hardly unknown to the more respectable residents of the great city. Brassaï photographed his bohemian subjects on streets and parks, as well as in bistros, bars, and nightclubs—the Bar de la Lune in Montmartre, the Cabaret des Fleurs in Montparnasse, and Le Monocle, also in Montparnasse, on the Boulevard Edgar-Quinet.

Le Monocle was owned and operated by that same Lucienne Franchi who later moved on to Montmartre (which explains why she is sometimes called Lulu de Montparnasse and sometimes Lulu de Montmartre). Lulu wore her short hair slicked back and dressed in men's clothes, at least from the waist up, often wearing a skirt rather than trousers to match her signature tuxedo jacket. Brassaï says that while there were a few small bars in 1930s Paris where women could meet other women, Le Monocle was one of the first nightclubs catering to a lesbian clientele—although straight people (like Brassaï, for example) were also welcome. Brassaï's discussion of lesbian love (written in the 1970s) is bound to strike the contemporary reader as benighted because of his assumption that same-sex love falls short not just of some heterosexual norm but of the masculine "ideal":

> From the owner, known as Lulu de Montparnasse, to the barmaid, from the waitress to the hat-check girl, all the women were dressed as men, and so totally masculine in appearance that at first glance one thought they were men. A tornado of virility has gusted through the place and blown away all the finery, all the tricks of feminine coquetry, changing women into boys, gangsters, policemen. Gone the trinkets, veils, ruffles! Obsessed by their unobtainable goal to be men, they wore the most somber uniforms: black tuxedos, as though in mourning for their ideal masculinity....And of course their hair—woman's crowning glory, abundant, waved, sweet-smelling, curled—had also been sacrificed on Sappho's altar.

Fortunately, the tone-deaf sense of female sexuality that Brassaï's prose conveys does not come across in his photographs, rightly acclaimed for their documentary depiction of Parisian nightlife, as in the one of Lulu chatting up a young woman at the bar of Le Monocle as another woman and the female bartender, both in male drag, look on.

Brassaï informs us that once Lulu moved on from Montparnasse to Montmartre, she "raised the standard of Sapphism in the Rue Pigalle," by which he means that she opened another lesbian nightclub. The move is noteworthy because the direction of bohemian migration in Paris after World War I (and even earlier) had been in the other direction—from Montmartre to Montparnasse. But unlike other locales that bohemians had been

9. All the people in Brassaï's photo of the nightclub scene at Le Monocle in Montparnasse are women, including Lulu, the owner of the establishment, on the left, as well as the elegantly dressed young woman on the right.

drawn to in the past, Montparnasse was not so much "a village in the heart of Paris" but a residential neighborhood whose urban geography did not mark it off from its surrounding environs, as the crooked streets of Greenwich Village sectioned that Bohemia off from the predominant New York City grid.

Indeed, Montparnasse was and is a rather ill-defined area, a single alleged *quartier* that nonetheless extends into two separate arrondissements, the sixth north of the Boulevard de Montparnasse and the fourteenth south of it. Several art academies, such as the École des Beaux-Arts, were located in the sixth arrondissement, while the fourteenth provided rows of low-rent rooms and studios, known as *cités des artistes*, to house the art students who studied at the academies. Montparnasse was also where scores of expatriate Americans settled after the war, including Gertrude Stein and her partner, Alice B. Toklas, whose apartment at 27, rue de Fleurus in the sixth arrondissement was an artistic destination not only for other expatriate Americans, such as Ernest Hemingway and F. Scott Fitzgerald, but also for painters who had migrated from Montmartre—notably Picasso— who were looking to Stein and other wealthy Americans to buy their work.

On first impression Montparnasse seems divided into a bourgeois half and a bohemian half, with the Boulevard de Montparnasse as the dividing line. While it is true that the academies that trained the artists, the journalists who reviewed their work, and the patrons who bought it all tended to live north of the boulevard whereas the artists who made the art lived south of it, what is more true is that the bourgeois-bohemian divide—never that definite anyway—really begins to break down in Montparnasse. André Warnod, the art critic who coined the term *L'École de Paris* (School of Paris), wrote in 1925 that artists were no longer "fierce enemies of the bourgeoisie," while at the same time members of high society "prided themselves on being 'up to the minute' and mingled with the artists." Perhaps the best examples of this beau monde or "beauhemian" element in Montparnasse are Peggy Guggenheim and Nancy Cunard, who both arrived in Paris in 1920 as advocates of the avant-garde, with Guggenheim lending her support mainly to modernist painters and Cunard backing surrealist writers. Both of these wealthy expatriate women, Guggenheim from America, Cunard from England, embraced the lax morality and excessive hedonism of Montparnasse Bohemia, but not all expatriates were so generous and accepting as they were.

Hemingway, for one, lambasted his fellow Americans when he was working as a foreign correspondent for the *Toronto Star*. In a dispatch titled "American Bohemians in Paris a Weird Lot" from March 1922, the young correspondent—who did not speak French—gets some basic facts wrong by locating Montparnasse in the Latin Quarter and confusing Baudelaire with Nerval as the nineteenth-century poet who walked a lobster on a leash. But he is right to suggest that the "work" required for one to be a bohemian might well interfere with the work of an artist:

> The scum of Greenwich Village, New York, has been skimmed off and deposited in large ladles on that section of Paris adjacent to the Café Rotonde. New scum, of course, has risen to take the place of the old, but the oldest scum, the thickest scum and scummiest scum has come across the ocean, somehow, and with its afternoon and evening levees has made the Rotonde the leading Latin Quarter [*sic*] showplace for tourists in search of atmosphere.
>
> Since the good old days when Charles Baudelaire led a purple lobster on a leash through the same old Latin Quarter, there has not been much good poetry written in cafés.... But the gang at the corner of the Boulevard Raspail have no time to work at anything else; they put in a full day at the Rotonde.

When he wrote this dispatch Hemingway had two addresses in the Latin Quarter, including a writing studio in the hotel where Verlaine had died, so perhaps he thought his was the more historically authentic Bohemia compared with the residential neighborhood of Montparnasse (where Hemingway himself would later move).

Hemingway is correct in observing that a number of Greenwich Village bohemians decamped to Paris, but he does not say why.

Certainly, the Red Scare of 1919–20 was one reason: Villagers sympathetic to communism found the political environs of Paris more welcoming than just about anywhere in the United States. At the same time, there seems to have been greater concord between art and ideology in pre-war New York than in post-war Paris. The disconnect between art and ideology is especially evident in the case of the surrealists, led by the poet André Breton, who tried to reconcile the economic theory of Karl Marx with the psychoanalytical theory of Sigmund Freud.

In 1930, the group published yet another entry in what seems like an interminable series of manifestoes, this one defending *L'âge d'or* (The golden age), a film by Luis Buñuel that includes any number of surrealist gags (like a man kicking a violin down the street and then stomping on the instrument) and ends by imagining Jesus Christ as the Duke de Blangis, the libertine antihero of the Marquis de Sade's *120 Days of Sodom*. The manifesto makes the strange claim that *L'âge d'or* shows the power of *amour fou* (mad, uncontrolled love) to overcome social injustice, a political position that is almost transcendently odd. The model for the coming politico-erotic revolution, the surrealists go on to explain, lies in the challenge to social convention posed by the Marquis de Sade. Although the final outcome of this challenge "remains to be seen," the result should be "the "triumph of the proletariat, which will mean the decomposition of class society." Perhaps unsurprisingly, the French Communist Party (PCF) was not persuaded and refused to heed surrealist overtures urging the PCF to combine recondite surrealist aesthetics with political action.

The buttoned-up Breton (nicknamed the "pope" of surrealism) seems a rather unlikely advocate for sexual liberation, long regarded as one of the most defining characteristics of Bohemia. A better representative of *amour fou* is the woman who may be the most influential female bohemian of all, Alice Ernestine Prin, better known as Kiki of Montparnasse. She is justly celebrated for her artistic collaboration with the surrealist photographer Man Ray, who used her face and body to form some of the most iconic images of the inter-war era. Kiki, however, was not just Ray's model and mistress but a considerable cultural figure in her own right.

An artist who drew and painted in a naïve style suggestive of Matisse, Kiki mounted successful shows at galleries on both the Left Bank in 1927 and on the Right Bank in 1930. In addition, she performed in Montparnasse nightspots like the Jockey Club, where she sang bawdy songs in a deadpan voice, including one said to be her favorite, a folk tune with new lyrics supplied by the surrealist poet Robert Desnos: "The young girls of Camaret say they are all virgins, / But when they are in bed they prefer my tool / more than a candle, / more than a candle...." In 1929, the 28-year-old Kiki published her memoirs, richly illustrated with Ray's nude photographs of the woman who by that time was widely known as "The Queen of Montparnasse."

When *Kiki Souvenirs* was published in an English translation in 1930, the book joined James Joyce's *Ulysses* (1922), D. H. Lawrence's *Lady Chatterley's Lover* (1928), and other works banned in the United States (and other countries) on supposed grounds of obscenity. No sooner did Kiki publish her memoires about her former career than she started on a new one, teaming up with the accordionist André Laroque in the early 1930s to sing professionally, more or less, in Montparnasse cabarets and bars, as well as recording several of her songs. Brassaï photographed her with Laroque and devoted several pages of appreciation to Kiki in *The Secret Paris of the '30s*, where he notes that her "skirt went up and down like a theatre curtain," sometimes revealing the complete absence of pubic hair (a condition known as pubic alopecia), which Kiki often disguised by touching up her armpits and pubis with a stick of charcoal. Brassaï also mentions the sad fact that addiction to alcohol and drugs made Kiki look like La Môme Bijou in later life and led to early death at the age of fifty-one, when she collapsed on the street outside her Montparnasse apartment.

In his rather mean-spirited introduction to *Kiki's Memoirs*, Hemingway asserted that the book should not and could not be translated (as if he would know). He is mostly generous, however, in his assessment of Kiki herself: "Having a fine face to start with she had made of it a work of art. She had a wonderfully beautiful body and a fine voice,... and she certainly dominated that era of Montparnasse more than Queen Victoria ever dominated the Victorian era." As for the era itself that Kiki dominated, Hemingway says that she "now looks like a monument to herself and to the era of Montparnasse that was definitely marked as closed" by the time Kiki published her book.

That assessment would have been news to Brassaï and to many others, for whom the freedom and energy of the Montparnasse Bohemia remained undiminished. What Hemingway probably means is that the era had ended for Americans. For most of the 1920s, Americans in Paris benefited from a very favorable currency exchange rate, but the value of the U.S. dollar against the French franc dropped considerably toward the end of the decade, when the French reversion to the gold standard in June 1928 and the Wall Street Crash of October 1929 effectively put an end to all the cheap expatriate living inter-war Americans had enjoyed in bohemian Montparnasse. Yet, even if Hemingway was right to suggest that Bohemia had become a thing of the past, that does not mean it had ended.

Chapter 5
The death of Bohemia

When Ernest Hemingway announced the death of Bohemia in 1930 after the Queen of Montparnasse published her memoirs, he was more than a half-century late to the funeral. In 1874, the Parisian journalist Firmin Maillard had already collected the remains of more than six dozen bohemians into the "common grave" of history: the cultural corpses named in Maillard's book *Les derniers bohèmes* (The last bohemians) include such well-known figures as Charles Baudelaire ("no man has recounted the disappointments of human life and nature with more magic") and obscure ones like Baptiste, the waiter at the Brasserie des Martyrs ("he worked side-by-side with great men"). A more recent occasion for the funeral rites of Bohemia was the centenary of Henry Murger's birth in 1922, which turned out to be an opportunity for declaring the death of Bohemia rather than celebrating Murger's accomplishments.

The novelist Lucien Descaves headed his newspaper tribute "La Fin de la Bohème" (The end of Bohemia), making the point that "the Latin Quarter is just a memory." He also quotes the brothers Edmond and Jules de Goncourt, novelists who also kept a detailed journal of their mordant observations, on Murger's "conversion" to a more stable existence: "He is rejecting Bohemia and passing over bag and baggage to the side of the gentleman of letters." Descaves quotes another passage in a similar vein from the

Goncourt journal: on the occasion of Murger's death in January 1861, the brothers recollect their last meeting with the man the previous month, when he was "gay and happy," having decided to make money the easy way, by writing for the stage. The Goncourts go on to reflect on the death of Murger as an event of "Biblical" proportions, portending the death of Bohemia itself:

> A death, when you think of it, which has something Biblical about it. It strikes me as the death of Bohemia, this death by decomposition, in which everything in Murger's life and the world which he depicted is combined: the orgies of work at night, the periods of poverty followed by periods of junketing, the neglected cases of pox, the ups and downs of existence without a home, the suppers instead of dinners, and the glasses of absinthe bringing consolation after a visit to a pawnshop; everything which wears a man out, burns him up, and finally kills him; a life opposed to all the principles of physical and spiritual hygiene, which results in a man dying in shreds at the age of forty-two, without enough strength in him left to suffer, and complaining of only one thing, the smell of rotten meat in his bedroom—the smell of his own body.

But Bohemia did not die with Murger in 1861, or in 1874, with the publication of Maillard's book, or in 1922, at the centenary of Murger's birth, or even in 1930, when Hemingway wrote that the era of Montparnasse had come to an end. However, something happened to Bohemia somewhere along the way that makes it seem different now than in the past.

Bohemia starts out as a kind of urban variant of Romanticism, and the Romantic reflex usually construes the past as preferable to the present—more authentic, less corrupted. That model of nostalgia, however, does not exactly work when it comes to Bohemia, because to wish for that earlier bohemian age would be to wish for the worst. Who really longs to return to the glory days of starvation and homelessness? In his 1922 reconsideration of

Bohemia Descaves made the common-sense observation that "poverty is humiliating."

One of the more striking things about the inter-war Montparnasse Bohemia that Kiki conveyed in her memoirs and that Brassaï documented in his photographs is how little either of them focused on the harshness of daily life. The world economy at the time was in the grip of the Great Depression, so by definition life was hard, but what comes across is not the hardship but the hedonism. One explanation for the change is obvious: impoverishment cannot be a distinguishing feature of Bohemia if entire societies are suffering from economic distress. Another explanation is the breakdown in the class division that separates bohemian and bourgeoisie. Although the boundary was never as absolute as bohemians claimed, the inter-war era makes the dissolution of that boundary abundantly clear, and not just in Montparnasse.

In Berlin during the late years of the Weimar Republic (1918–33), the bohemian lifestyle was taken up—if only at the end of the working day or on the weekend—by large numbers of ordinary, middle-class people, especially among the younger generation. The phenomenon was only one effect of the "class slippage" that the novelist Arthur Landsberger observed in 1929: "Individuals slip out of…their class. When the well-situated bourgeois child slips out, he becomes a bohemian"—or worse (Landsberger's essay concerns the social makeup of Berlin's criminal underworld).

But if Berlin's Bohemia gained social adherents during the Weimar era as an expression of the modern lifestyle, it lost aesthetic adherents because it was no longer new, or, at least, not new enough for modernism (in contrast to Montmartre's Bohemia a quarter-century before). The architect Hannes Meyer, who would go on to direct the Bauhaus design school from 1928 to 1930, wrote in 1926 that "[y]esterday is dead: dead, the bohemian," as well as the aesthetic so beloved by bohemian artists and writers: "Dead, the artwork as a 'thing in itself,' as 'L'art pour l'art': our collective consciousness tolerates no individual excess." Although Meyer probably does not have fascism in mind when he says "collective consciousness," once Adolf Hitler came to power in January 1933 all forms of "individual excess," bohemian or otherwise, could have no place in the totalitarian state that emerged after the collapse of the Weimar Republic.

In the run up to World War II, the combination of mass politics and economic depression assured the temporary demise of Bohemia, but the sense of impending catastrophe also fueled some last-gasp moments of bohemian exuberance, especially in Paris prior to German occupation (May 1940–December 1944). The cliché that has pre-war hedonists "dancing on the edge of the volcano," however hackneyed, conveys a measure of truth. The expression dates to December 1928 and is more correctly rendered simply as "dancing on a volcano." The German foreign minister Gustav Stresemann coined the phrase when he was in negotiations with the Western powers over Germany's war debt, seeking to mitigate the onerous terms of the Treaty of Versailles. "Germany gives a false impression of prosperity," Stresemann explained. "The economic position is only flourishing on the surface. Germany is in fact dancing on a volcano."

The diplomat's striking metaphor describing the perilous economic circumstances of Germany in the late 1920s can also be applied to the social, cultural, and political conditions of the late 1930s. As the world careened toward war, the days of the bohemians were numbered, and when the volcano erupted with the Munich Accords, Hitler's annexation of Austria, the invasion of Poland, and the rest, their number ran out. Bohemians may not lead a regular, stable existence, but they require, nonetheless, that the broader society be stable enough to make their individual instability possible.

All bohemians—perhaps without knowing it—depend on the financial health of the larger economy in order to live their déclassé lives. Simply stated, anyone who lives on credit counts on the economic well-being of the creditor who extends the credit in the first place. Indeed, it would not be until after World War II that social and economic conditions would improve to the point that bohemians could once again enjoy the freedom to reject society and elect impoverishment. In the United States, the necessary regimentation of the war years spilled over into the peacetime economy of the 1950s, as thousands of G.I.'s traded in their camouflage outfits for grey flannel suits, a uniform of a different sort that helped them blend into the corporate economy and the conformist society. If ever conditions were ripe for the revival of Bohemia, this was it: not since 1830s France had society produced such a profusion of bourgeois values as did 1950s America.

The counterculture reaction to 1950s conformism came in several varieties, perhaps most famously as the Beat Generation, which included the poets Allen Ginsberg and Gary Snyder; the novelists William Burroughs and Jack Kerouac; and several other key figures, notably Neal Cassady, whose wildly spontaneous, liberated behavior served as inspiration for the main members of the Beats, especially for Kerouac. His novel *On the Road* is a roman à clef featuring fictional versions of several members of the loosely affiliated group, as in the description of the first meeting of Dean Moriarty (Cassady) and Carlo Marx (Ginsberg): "A tremendous thing happened when Dean met Carlo Marx. Two keen minds they are, they took to each other at the drop of a hat. Two piercing eyes glanced into two piercing eyes—the holy con-man with the shining mind, and the sorrowful poetic con-man with the dark mind that is Carlo Marx.... [T]hey danced down the streets like dingledodies, and I shambled after...."

The use of clichés like "drop of a hat" and invented words like "dingledodies" reflects the loose improvisational style of the novel, written over a period of three weeks in April 1951, originally typed onto one continuous roll of paper but later retyped onto four hundred regular pages. The spontaneous style practiced by Kerouac and other members of the Beat Generation—in both art and life—also reflects the influence of bebop, the type of jazz pioneered in the 1940s by the saxophonist Charlie Parker, the trumpeter Dizzy Gillespie, the pianist Thelonious Monk, and others. In fact, the term *beat* in "Beat Generation" is often said to derive from the complex rhythms of bebop jazz, although it may also convey a sense of exhaustion, of being "beaten down" by established society.

While there can be no doubt that the members of the Beat Generation have much in common with the bohemian tradition—the cultivation of new forms of artistic expression, the refusal of conventional morality, the indulgence in alcohol and drugs—they also depart from that tradition is some significant ways. Gone is the association with a bohemian-friendly neighborhood of a major metropolis: the Beat Generation spread themselves all over the United States—and Mexico—with some members spending time in New York City, others in San Francisco, still others in Denver, Colorado, and so on.

As for bohemian removal from the bourgeoisie, most of the Beat Generation had solid middle-class origins, and while the porousness of class is nothing new in the history of Bohemia, the middle-class pedigree of much of the Beat Generation is striking (with some exceptions, like Snyder, who came from an impoverished farming family). Kerouac and Ginsberg, who met when they were students at Columbia University in New York, may have come from relatively modest backgrounds in Lowell, Massachusetts, and Paterson, New Jersey, respectively, but they were hardly poor. Burroughs, by contrast, came from a wealthy family.

But the economic background of the Beat Generation says less, perhaps, about their "qualifications" as authentic bohemians than it does about how much the nature of Bohemia had changed since its mythic origins in Murger's Paris. In this context, the relatively straightforward implications of the word *generation* are more germane to the change than the ambiguities of the word *beat*. After all, the counterculture sensibility of the Beat Generation ramified into post-war American society on a scale hitherto unseen, and when teenagers in the suburbs begin to play bongo drums while wearing sunglasses and black turtlenecks, not to mention watching the beatnik character Maynard G. Krebs (played by Bob Denver) crack wise in jazz lingo on the TV sitcom *The Many Loves of Dobie Gillis* (1959–63), then we can be sure that while we may not be in Kansas anymore, Bohemia clearly is.

Not all of that post-war generation known as Baby Boomers felt the counterculture allure of the Beats, but many did, and many more wound up deeply invested in the counterculture of the 1960s, especially in their college years, when their education was colored by the tie-dyed hues of drug, sex, and rock 'n' roll, as well as by protest against the Vietnam War and other American misadventures. Although there is much about this generation that does not chime with Bohemia writ large (notably the impulse to activism, rarely practiced by the bohemians of old), as they matured and became absorbed into the mainstream they professed to oppose, their purchasing power drove commercial culture in new directions, leading the journalist David Brooks to describe them in broad sociological terms as "bourgeois bohemians," or "Bobos."

Brooks published *Bobos in Paradise* in 2000, taking stock of how much American society had changed since only 1995 or so. He found it increasingly difficult to distinguish hip bohemian from square bourgeois: "It was now impossible to tell an espresso-sipping artist from a cappuccino-gulping banker. And this wasn't just a matter of fashion accessories. I found that if you investigated people's attitude toward sex, morality, leisure time, and work, it was getting harder and harder to separate the antiestablishment renegade from the pro-establishment company man." Distinguishing the bohemian artist from the bourgeois banker is harder now because the American economy has evolved away from industrial production and toward personal service. These days, art comes close to being a service like any other, however much the art school graduate who works as a barista in a coffee shop might resist the idea of the artist as a service provider.

If the original bohemians emerged out of a sense of alienation from and revulsion over the propertied classes whose power derived from an industrial economy, the attenuation of that economy would seem to likewise entail the attenuation of the bohemian "class" as well. But as Brooks observes, the bohemian appears not to have vanished from the contemporary urban scene so much as to have been transformed into something else, variously termed—in addition to Bobo—"boburbian" (suburban bohemian), "neobohemian," and "fauxhemian." At the root of these various formulations lies the relationship between the bohemian and the commercial culture of capitalist economies.

From the capitalist perspective, bohemianism has served as a marketing strategy to sell a certain lifestyle formerly associated with the counterculture (that's the Bobo phenomenon in a nutshell). From a bohemian perspective, sociocultural marginalization and opposition to the capitalist economy can be exploited and monetized, so long as the outsider entrepreneur manages to maintain the identity of outsider and markets to other outsiders: to sell without selling out (that's the neobohemian phenomenon in a nutshell). That neobohemian paradox reveals only one of the numerous ways that the myth of Bohemia has been transformed and adapted to economic and cultural conditions that are very different from those that gave birth to the myth.

Perhaps Bohemia today is not dead so much as moribund, or, at the very least, tired. If so, the sense of bohemian exhaustion may have its finest artistic representation in *Boheemielämää* (Bohemian life, 1992), a mordant tragicomedy directed by the Finnish filmmaker Aki Kaurismäki that captures perfectly just how belated the bohemian myth seems today. Bohemia is traditionally the country of youth, but Kaurismäki's hangdog bohemians are all middle-aged. Known outside of Finland as *La Vie de Bohéme*, the French-language film is both an homage to and a commentary on Murger's *Scenes of Bohemian Life*.

Kaurismäki sets the film in contemporary Paris, but not in the Latin Quarter or other neighborhoods frequented by Murger's bohemians. Rather, the action is set in Malakoff and Ivry-sur-Seine, two of the *banlieues rouges* (red suburbs) on the outskirts of Paris so called because of the dominance of the French Communist Party in local politics. The change of locale makes

10. Kaurismäki's bohemians seem as worn out and exhausted as the myth of Bohemia itself: from left, Mimi, Rodolfo, Marcel, Musette, and Schaunard. Mimi holds one of Rodolfo's "masterpieces."

sense because the bohemian environs of Murger's day are upscale now, so the down-market banlieues chime with the limited means available to Rodolfo, Marcel, and Schaunard. Colline is missing from the group, and the writer Marcel, whose last name is now Marx, has swapped arts with Rodolfo, now a painter from Albania with a beautiful black Laika (a Russian dog breed) named Baudelaire.

Rodolfo begins his affair with Mimi soon after she shows up at the door of an apartment adjoining his, expecting to spend the night with a girlfriend. The girlfriend has moved without telling her, so Rodolfo, acting the gentleman, offers Mimi his place and leaves to spend the night "with friends." In fact, he sleeps in the Montmartre Cemetery; in the morning, as he leaves he tosses a bunch of flowers onto the grave of none other than Henry Murger. That bit of homage is obviously an addition to the traditional narrative, but for the most part the black-and-white film faithfully recounts the main stories from Murger's book and many of the small ones, including the café scene featuring the bicephalous rabbit. In Kaurismäki's visually inventive retelling, the two-headed rabbit becomes a two-headed trout that Rodolfo halves and shares with Marcel.

The Romeo and Juliet story featuring Rodolphe in the book is given to Schaunard in the film when he drives up with a ladder on the top of his Reliant Robin (a three-wheeled micro-coupe) with plans to romance his Juliet. That romance is cut short when Marcel gets a call from Rodolfo, who has been deported back to Albania but is at the French border, asking for help to reenter the country illegally. The two bohemians drive to the border and pick him up. Back in Paris, Rodolfo is reunited with Baudelaire since Mimi is temporarily out of the picture, having taken up with another man. But she returns to him soon enough.

Rodolfo finds success as Marcel does in the book by painting a portrait of a sugar magnate who also fancies himself a collector and buys Rodolfo's masterpiece, *The Crossing of the Red Sea*. Rodolfo later finds the painting in a shop window, altered to advertise sugar. After a thief picks his pocket on the Métro, the newly impoverished Rodolfo cannot provide for Mimi, so she leaves him again. Come winter, she returns one last time, deathly ill, and is put in a private room in the hospital, which the three bohemian friends pay for by selling what they have: Marcel his books, Rodolfo his paintings, and Schaunard his Reliant Robin. Mimi lasts until the spring, when she asks Rodolfo to pick some flowers for her room. He does so, but when he returns Mimi is dead. He drops the bouquet and walks slowly out of the hospital, as the mournful sound of Toshitake Shinohara's song "Yukino Furu Machio" (Snow-covered town) covers his exit, continuing to play over the end titles.

However many liberties Kaurismäki may take with Murger, they are justified by his fidelity to the spirit of *Scenes of Bohemian Life*: the pathos, the humor, and the dedication—not to art so much as to the art of living. The film goes a long way toward recovering the historical origins of Bohemia by retelling Murger's tales in a playfully respectful way, while also situating Murger's bohemians in a contemporary urban context that comes across as credible. If Rodolphe, Marcel, and Schaunard had followed their hopeless artistic dreams in the Paris of the early 1990s, this is where they would be—in the run-down neighborhood on the outskirts of the city, not in the tourist-infested Latin Quarter.

At the same time, the film suggests that it is not just the neighborhood that is run-down, but the myth of Bohemia itself. Given how exhausted the myth seems today, we might say of the death of Bohemia what the Russian author Lou-Andreas Salomé said of the death of God. Improving on Fredrich Nietzsche's notorious claim that "God is dead," Salomé added that while God had indeed died, He nonetheless continues to have a cultural afterlife. As with the death of God, it may not be possible to say precisely when the death of Bohemia occurred—only that it has, and that, ever since, its cultural afterlife has continued to take various forms, some seemingly earnest, like the movie musical

Rent, and some ironic, like *Boheemielämää.* How long this moribund Bohemia will continue its cultural afterlife is hard to say, but once it ends, the bohemians themselves—whether called Bobos, boburbians, fauxhemians, neobohemians, or something else—will be the last to acknowledge its passing.

References

Introduction

Raymond Williams, *Keywords: A Vocabulary of Culture and Society* (New York: Oxford University Press, 1985), 46.

Charles Baudelaire, *Intimate Journals*, trans. Christopher Isherwood (San Francisco: City Lights, 1983), 86.

Pierre Bourdieu, *The Rules of Art: Genesis and Structure of the Literary Field*, trans. Susan Emanuel (Stanford, CA: Stanford University Press, 1996), 134, 55.

Vic Gatrell, *The First Bohemians: Life and Art in London's Golden Age* (London: Allen Lane, 2013), xi.

Robert Darnton, introduction to Anne Gédéon Lafitte, marquis de Pelleport, *The Bohemians*, trans. Vivien Folkenflik (Philadelphia: University of Pennsylvania Press, 2010), ix–xliii.

George Sand, *Story of My Life: The Autobiography of George Sand*, ed. Thelma Jurgrau (Albany: State University of New York Press, 1991), 907, 893.

George Sand, *Horace*, trans. Zack Rogrow (San Francisco: Mercury House, 1995), 269.

George Sand, *The Last Aldini: A Love Story* (Philadelphia: B. Peterson and Brothers, 1871), 18.

Box

Félix Pyat, "Les artistes," *Nouveau tableau de Paris au XIXme siècle: Paris moderne* (Paris: Charles-Béchet, 1834), 4:6–7, 8–9, 10–11. Translation mine.

Chapter 1

Arthur Groos and Roger Parker, *Giacomo Puccini: "La bohème"* (Cambridge: Cambridge University Press, 1986), 32.

George Sand, *The Last Aldini: A Love Story* (Philadelphia: B. Peterson and Brothers, 1871), 34, 46, 44, 77.

Honoré de Balzac, *Muse of the Department, A Prince of Bohemia, and Other Stories*, trans. Janes Warring and Jno. Rudd (Philadelphia: Gebb, 1899), 5, 13, 22, 39, 40, 2–3.

Alexander Garvin, *What Makes a Great City* (Washington, D.C.: Island Press, 2016), 62.

Henry Murger, *Scenes from the Latin Quarter* (London: Capuchin Classics, 2010), 20, 46, 133, 32.

Henry Murger, *Scènes de la vie de Bohême*, 3rd ed. (Paris: Michel Lévy, 1852), 69.

William Shakespeare, *Romeo and Juliet* (3.5.1–2, 6), *The Oxford Shakespeare: The Complete Works*, 2nd ed., ed. Stanley Wells and Gary Taylor (Oxford: Oxford University Press, 2005), 389.

Murger, *Scenes from the Latin Quarter*, 305, 231, 25, 238, 246, 252, 255.

Robert Baldick, *The First Bohemian: The Life of Henry Murger* (London: Hamish Hamilton, 1961), 118.

Théodore Barrièrre and Henry Murger, *Bohemia or, La Bohème*, trans. Frank J. Morlock ([N.P:] Borgo Press, 2012), 20, 208, 214, 217, 231, 235, 236.

Baldick, *Henry Murger*, 123.

Giacomo Puccini, *La Bohème*, trans. Ellen H. Bleiler (New York: Dover, 1984), 6, 62, 75.

Alexandra Wilson, *Puccini's "La Bohème"* (Oxford: Oxford University Press, 2021), 58, 59.

Thomas Beecham, *A Mingled Chime: An Autobiography* (New York: Greenwood Press, 1976), 78.

Mordaunt Hall, "Brilliant Acting and Excellent Stage Settings in King Vidor's 'La Boheme,'" *New York Times*, March 7, 1926, section 8, p. 5.

Rent, directed by Chris Columbus (2005; Culver City, CA: Sony Pictures Home Entertainment, 2006), DVD.

Ben Brantley, "Enter Singing: Young, Hopeful, and Taking on the Big Time," *New York Times*, section C, p. 13.

Murger, *Scenes from the Latin Quarter*, 20.

Box

George Sand, *The Last Aldini: A Love Story* (Philadelphia: B. Peterson and Brothers, 1871), 20, 48, 95.

Chapter 2

Honoré de Balzac, *Muse of the Department, A Prince of Bohemia, and Other Stories*, trans. Janes Warring and Jno. Rudd (Philadelphia: Gebb, 1899), 2:13.

Norma Evanson, "Paris, 1890–1940," in *Metropolis: 1890–1940*, ed. Anthony Sutcliffe (Chicago: University of Chicago Press, 1984), 262.

Henry Murger, *Scenes from the Latin Quarter* (London: Capuchin Classics, 2010), 94, 134–35, 58.

Giacomo Puccini, *La Bohème*, trans. Ellen H. Bleiler (New York: Dover, 1984), 13.

Théophile Gautier, *Portraits contemporains*, 3rd ed. (Paris: Charpentier, 1874), 134–35. Translation mine.

Richard Holmes, introduction to Théophile Gautier, *My Fantoms*, trans. Richard Holmes (New York: New York Review of Books, 2008), xvii.

Théophile Gautier, *Portraits et souvenirs littéraires* (Paris: Michel Lévy, 1875), 40. Translation mine.

Richard Holmes, *Footsteps: Adventures of a Romantic Biographer* (New York: Vintage, 1985), 213.

Champfleury, *Les Vignettes romantiques: Histoire de la littérature et de l'art, 1825–1840* (Paris: E. Dentu, 1883), 166.

Joanna Richardson, *The Bohemians: La Vie de Bohème in Paris 1830–1914* (South Brunswick, NJ: A. S. Barnes, 1969), 58.

Quoted by Marcus Boon, *The Road of Excess: A History of Writers on Drugs* (Cambridge, MA: Harvard University Press, 2002), 134–5, 136.

Enid Starkie, *Baudelaire* (New York: New Directions, 1958), 61.

Quoted by Joanna Richardson, *Baudelaire: A Biography* (New York: St. Martins, 1994), 83.

Orlo Williams, *Vie de Bohème: A Patch of Romantic Paris* (Boston: Richard G. Badger, 1913), 231–32.

Charles Baudelaire, *The Flowers of Evil*, trans. James McGowan (Oxford: Oxford University Press, 1993).

Charles Baudelaire, *The Painter of Modern Life and Other Essays*, 2nd ed., trans. Jonathan Mayne (London: Phaidon, 1995), 28–29.

Quoted by Joanna Levin and Edward Whitey, "Bohemianism," *Walt Whitman in Context*, ed. Joanna Levin and Edward Whitey (Cambridge: Cambridge University Press, 2018), 208.

Walt Whitman, "The Two Vaults," *"Leaves of Grass" and Other Writings*, ed. Michael Moon (New York: Norton, 2002), 576.

"Bohemia in New-York," *New York Times*, January 6, 1858, 4.

William Dean Howells, *Literary Friends and Acquaintances: A Personal Retrospect of American Authorship* (1900; New York: Harper & Brothers, 1911), 69.

J. Barbey d'Aurevilly, *Les oeuvres et les hommes* (Paris: Amyot, 1865), 4:339–40. Translation mine.

Albert Parry, *Garrets and Pretenders: A History of Bohemianism in America* (New York: Covici, Fried, 1933), 214–16.

John Taylor Williams, *The Shores of Bohemia: A Cape Cod Story, 1910–1960* (New York: Farrar, Straus and Giroux, 2022), 16.

Donald E. Pitzer, ed., *America's Communal Utopias* (Chapel Hill, NC: University of North Carolina Press, 1997), 457, 420, 413, 165.

Quoted by Robert E. Norton, *Secret Germany: Stefan George and his Circle* (Ithaca, NY: Cornell University Press, 2002), 150.

Quoted by Carol Diethe, *Nietzsche's Women: Beyond the Whip* (Berlin: Walter de Gruyter, 1996), 125.

Norton, *Secret Germany*, 332, 153.

Théophile Gautier, preface to *Mademoiselle de Maupin*, trans. Joanna Richardson (New York: Penguin, 1981), 51.

Robert Baldick, *The First Bohemian: The Life of Henry Murger* (London: Hamish Hamilton, 1961), 11–12, 106.

Boxes

Gérard Nerval, *Petits châteaux de bohême* (Paris: Didier, 1853), 7–9. Translation mine.

F. Gräfin zu Reventlow, *Herrn Dames Aufzeichnungen; oder Begebenheiten aus einem merkwürdigen Stadtteil* (Munich: Langen, 1913), 122–23, 130–31. Translation mine.

Chapter 3

Karl Marx, *Der achtzehnte Brumaire des Louis Bonaparte* (Hamburg: Meißner, 1885), 65. Translation mine.

Karl Marx, *Later Political Writings*, ed. and trans. Terrell Carver (Cambridge: Cambridge University Press, 1996), 31, 77–78.

Alexandre Schanne, *Souvenirs de Schaunard* (Paris: Charpentier, 1887), 204.

"Vous n'êtes pas un bohème, mais la bohème." Quoted by Luc Sante, *The Other Paris* (New York: Farrar, Straus and Giroux, 2015), 152.

A[lexandre] Privat d'Anglemont, *Paris Inconnu* (Paris: Delahays, 1861), 53, 46, 18, 133–35, 35, 20–21, 18.

Frederick Engels, preface to Karl Marx, *The Paris Commune* (New York: New York Labor News Company, 1902), 20.

Rupert Christiansen, *Paris Babylon: The Story of the Paris Commune* (New York: Viking, 1995), 298.

Jerrold Siegel, *Bohemian Paris: Culture, Politics, and the Boundaries of Bourgeois Life* (New York: Penguin, 1987), 181.

Marx, *Later Political Writings*, 189, 195.

Quoted by Matei Calinescu, *Five Faces of Modernity: Modernism, Avant-Garde, Decadence, Kitsch, Postmodernism* (Durham, NC: Duke University Press, 1987), 102.

Sante, *The Other Paris*, 154.

Quoted by Richard D. Sonn, *Anarchism and Cultural Politics in Fin de Siècle France* (Lincoln: University of Nebraska Press, 1989), 68–69.

Jean Émile-Bayard, *Montmartre Past and Present*, trans. Ralph Anningson and Tutor Davies (New York: Brentano's, [1929]), 116, 132.

Floyd Dell, *Looking at Life* (New York: Knopf, 1924), 67, 125, 67.

Floyd Dell, *Homecoming: An Autobiography* (New York: Farrar and Rinehart, 1933), 246.

Parry, *Garrets and Pretenders*, 271.

Max Eastman, *Enjoyment of Living* (New York: Harpers, 1948), 394.

The Masses 5.1 (October 1913): 2.

Dell, *Homecoming*, 247.

[Margaret Sanger], "The Aim," *The Woman Rebel* 1, no. 1 (March 1914): 1–2.

Crystal Eastman, "Birth Control in the Feminist Program," *The Birth Control Review* 2 (January 1918): 3.

Timothy J. Gilfoyle, *City of Eros: New York City, Prostitution, and the Commercialization of Sex, 1790–1920* (New York: Norton, 1992), 187.

Dell, *Homecoming*, 252.

Margaret Sanger, *The Autobiography of Margaret Sanger* (Mineola, NY: Dover, 2004), 121, 262.

"Army Ousts Masses Editor," *New York Times*, July 17, 1918, 8.

Claude McKay, *A Long Way from Home*, ed. Gene Andrew Jarrett (New Brunswick, NJ: Rutgers University Press, 2007), 28

Claude McKay, "If We Must Die," *The Liberator* 2, no. 7 (July 1919): 21.

Robert K. Murray, *Red Scare: A Study in National Hysteria, 1919-1920* (Minneapolis: University of Minnesota Press, 1955), 178.

Claude McKay, "Roman Holliday," *The Liberator* 2, no. 7 (July 1919): 21.

Max Eastman, introduction to Claude McKay, *Harlem Shadows* (New York: Harcourt, Brace and Company, 1922), ix, xv.

Carl Van Vechten, *Parties: Scenes from Contemporary New York Life* (New York: Knopf, 1930), 29.

Floyd Dell, "Alcoholiday," *The Masses* 8, no. 8 (June 1916): 30.

Chapter 4

Gustave Courbet to Francis and Marie Wey, July 31, 1850, *Letters of Gustave Courbet*, ed. Petra ten-Doesschate Chu (Chicago: University of Chicago Press, 1992), 98–99.

Émile Zola, *L'Assommoir*, trans. Margaret Mauldon (Oxford: Oxford University Press, 1995), 251.

"Montmartre, an authentic village in the heart of Paris," Paris Convention and Visitors Bureau, 2015. https://en.parisinfo.com/discovering-paris/walks-in-paris/montmartre-village-in-paris.

Sue Roe, *In Montmartre: Picasso, Matisse, and the Birth of Modernist Art* (New York: Penguin, 2014), 92–93.

Richard D. Sonn, "Marginality and Transgression: Anarchy's Subversive Allure," *Montmartre and the Making of Mass Culture*, ed. Gabriel P. Weisberg (New Brunswick, NJ: Rutgers University Press, 2001), 130.

Roe, *In Montmartre*, 39.

Félicien Fagus [Georges-Eugène Faillet], "L'Invasion espagnole: Picasso," *La Revue blanche* 25, no. 195 (July 15, 1901), 464–65.

Yvette Guilbert, *Autres temps, autres chants* (Paris: Laffont, 1946), 59. Translation mine.

Jean-Émile-Bayard, *Montmartre: Past and Present*, trans. Ralph Anningson and Tudor Davis (New York: Brentano's, [1926]), 158.

Harold B. Segel, *Turn-of-the-Century Cabaret: Paris, Barcelona, Berlin, Munich, Vienna, Cracow, Moscow, St. Petersburg, Zurich* (New York: Columbia University Press, 1987), 60–61.

Sante, *The Other Paris*, 183.

Maurice Verne, *Les Amuseurs de Paris* (Paris: Éditions de France, 1932), 182. Translation mine.

Carolyn Burke, *No Regrets: The Life of Edith Piaf* (London: Bloomsbury, 2011), 32.

Margaret Crosland, *Piaf* (New York: Putnam's, 1985), 42.

Brassaï, *The Secret Paris of the '30s*, trans. Richard Miller (New York: Random House, 1976), n.p.

André Warnod, *Les Berceaux de la jeune peinture: Montmartre, Montparnasse* (Paris: Albin Michel, 1925), 186. Translation mine.

Ernest Hemingway, "American Bohemians in Paris," *Dateline Toronto: The Complete Toronto Star Dispatches*, ed. William White (New York: Scribner Classics, 1985), 148–50.

Ernest Hemingway, *A Moveable Feast: The Restored Edition* (New York: Scribner, 2009), 16.

The Surrealist Group, "Manifesto of the Surrealists concerning *L'Âge d'or*, in *The Shadow and Its Shadow: Surrealist Writings on the Cinema*, ed. Paul Hammond, 3rd ed. (San Francisco: City Lights, 2000), 189.

Billy Klüver and Julie Martin, foreword to *Kiki's Memoirs* (Hopewell, NJ: Echo Press, 1996), 22.

Brassaï, *The Secret Paris of the '30s*, n.p.

Ernest Hemingway, introduction to *Kiki's Memoirs*, 50, 47.

Boxes

Maurice Lefèvre, "Les gestes de la chanson," *Le journal pour tous* 29 (July 15, 1896): 6. Translation mine.

Arthur Symons, *Colour Studies in Paris* (London: Chapman and Hall, 1918), 81–82.

Afterword

Fermin Maillard, *Les Derniers Bohèmes: Henri Murger et son temps* (Paris: Sartorius, 1874), 136, 269. Translation mine.

Lucien Descaves, "La Fin de la Bohème: La conversion de Murger," *L'Intransigeant*, March 26, 1922, 1. Translation mine.

Robert Baldick, ed. and trans., *Pages from the Goncourt Journal* (Harmondsworth: Penguin, 1984), 57.

Descaves, "La Fin de la Bohème," 1.

Arthur Landsberger, "The Berlin Underworld," *The Weimar Republic Sourcebook*, ed. Anton Kaes et al. (Berkeley: University of California Press, 1994), 732.

Hannes Meyer, "The New World," *The Weimar Republic Sourcebook*, 448.

Eric Sutton, ed. and trans., *Gustav Stresemann: His Diaries, Letters, and Papers* (New York: Macmillan, 1940), 3:405–6.

Jack Kerouac, *On the Road*, in *Road Novels 1957–1960*, ed. Douglas Brinkley (New York: Library Classics of the United States, 2007), 7.

David Brooks, *Bobos in Paradise: The New Upper Class and How They Got There* (New York: Simon & Schuster, 2000), 10.

Angela Livingstone, *Salomé: Her Life and Work* (Mount Kisco, NY: Moyer Bell, 1984), 74–75.

Further reading

Aronson, Amy. *Crystal Eastman: A Revolutionary Life*. New York: Oxford University Press, 2020.

Bakewell, Michael. *Fitzrovia: London's Bohemia*. London: National Portrait Gallery, 1999.

Baldick, Robert. *The First Bohemian: The Life of Henry Murger*. London: Hamish Hamilton, 1961.

Barnet, Andrea. *All-Night Party: The Women of Bohemian Greenwich Village and Harlem, 1913–1930*. Chapel Hill, NC: Algonquin Books, 2004.

Baudelaire, Charles. *The Painter of Modern Life and Other Essays*. 2nd ed. Translated by Jonathan Mayne. London: Phaidon, 1995.

Benjamin, Walter. *The Writer of Modern Life: Essays on Charles Baudelaire*. Edited by Michael William. Cambridge, MA: Harvard University Press, 2006.

Bingham, Shawn Chandler, and Lindsey A. Freeman, eds. *The Bohemian South: Creating Countercultures, from Poe to Punk*. Chapel Hill: University of North Carolina Press, 2017.

Boon, Marcus. *The Road of Excess: A History of Writers on Drugs*. Cambridge, MA: Harvard University Press, 2002.

Bourdieu, Pierre. *The Rules of Art: Genesis and Structure of the Literary Field*. Translated by Susan Emanuel. Stanford, CA: Stanford University Press, 1996.

Brassaï. *The Secret Paris of the '30s*. Translated by Richard Miller. New York: Random House, 1976.

Brooker, Peter. *Bohemia in London: The Social Scene of Early Modernism* (Basingstoke: Palgrave Macmillan, 2004.

Brooks, David. *Bobos in Paradise: The New Upper Class and How They Got There*. New York: Simon & Schuster, 2000.

Brown, Marilyn R. *Gypsies and Other Bohemians: The Myth of the Artist in Nineteenth-Century France*. Ann Arbor, MI: UMI Research Press, 1985.

Buhle, Paul, et al. *Bohemians: A Graphic History*. London: Verso, 2014.

Burke, Carolyn. *No Regrets: The Life of Edith Piaf*. London: Bloomsbury, 2011.

Calinescu, Matei. *Five Faces of Modernity: Modernism, Avant-Garde, Decadence, Kitsch, Postmodernism*. Durham, NC: Duke University Press, 1987.

Christiansen, Rupert. *Paris Babylon: The Story of the Paris Commune*. New York: Viking, 1995.

Coffield, Darren. *Tales from the Colony Room: Soho's Lost Bohemia*. London: Unbound, 2020.

Cottom, Daniel. *International Bohemia: Scenes of Nineteenth-Century Life*. Philadelphia: University of Pennsylvania Press, 2013.

Darnton, Robert. *The Literary Underground of the Old Regime*. Cambridge, MA: Harvard University Press, 1982.

David, Hugh. *The Fitzrovians: Portrait of Bohemian London, 1900–55*. London: Sceptre, 1989.

Dell, Floyd. *Homecoming: An Autobiography*. New York: Farrar and Rinehart, 1933.

Dell, Floyd. *Looking at Life*. New York: Knopf, 1924.

Eastman, Max. *Enjoyment of Living*. New York: Harpers, 1948.

Easton, Malcolm. *Artists and Writers in Paris: The Bohemian Idea, 1803–1867*. London: Edward Arnold, 1964.

Émile-Bayard, Jean. *Montmartre Past and Present*. Translated by Ralph Anningson and Tutor Davies. New York: Brentano's, [1929].

Frank, Dan. *Bohemian Paris: Picasso, Modigliani, Matisse, and the Birth of Modern Art*. Translated by Cynthia Hope Liebow. New York: Grove Press, 2001.

Gatheral, James. *The Bohemia Republic: Transnational Literary Networks in the Nineteenth Century*. New York: Routledge, 2021.

Gatrell, Vic. *The First Bohemians: Life and Art in London's Golden Age*. London: Allen Lane, 2013.

Gordon, Mel. *Horizontal Collaboration: The Erotic World of Paris, 1920–1946*. Port Townsend, WA: Feral House, 2015.

Graña, César. *Bohemian versus Bourgeois: French Society and the French Man of Letters in the Nineteenth Century*. New York: Basic Books, 1964.

Graña, Cesar, and Marigay Graña, eds. *On Bohemia: The Code of the Self-Exiled*. New Brunswick, NJ: Transaction, 1990.

Groos, Arthur, and Roger Parker. *Giacomo Puccini: "La bohème."* Cambridge: Cambridge University Press, 1986.

Hahn, Emily. *Romantic Rebels: An Informal History of Bohemianism in America*. Boston: Houghton Mifflin, 1967.

Hemingway, Ernest. *A Moveable Feast: The Restored Edition*. New York: Scribner, 2009.

Hewitt, Nicholas. *Montmartre: A Cultural History*. Liverpool: Liverpool University Press, 2020.

Hibbitt, Richard, ed. *Other Capitals of the Nineteenth Century: An Alternative Mapping of Literary and Cultural Space*. New York: Palgrave Macmillan, 2017.

Hofstadter, Richard. *Anti-Intellectualism in American Life*. New York: Vintage, 1963.

Huddleston, Sisley, *Bohemian Literary and Social Life in Paris: Salons, Cafés, Studios*. London: Harrap, 1928.

Humphrey, Robert E. *Children of Fantasy: The First Rebels of Greenwich Village*. New York: Wiley, 1978.

Hussey, Andrew. *Paris: The Secret History*. New York: Bloomsbury, 2006.

Kaes, Anton, et al. *The Weimar Republic Sourcebook*. Berkeley: University of California Press, 1994.

Klüver, Billy, and Julie Martin, eds. *Kiki's Memoirs*. Hopewell, NJ: Echo Press, 1996.

Lause, Mark A. *The Antebellum Crisis and America's First Bohemians*. Kent, OH: Kent State University Press, 2009.

Levin, Joanna. *Bohemia in America, 1858–1920*. Stanford, CA: Stanford University Press, 2010.

Lloyd, Richard. *Neo-Bohemia: Art and Commerce in the Postindustrial City*. New York: Routledge, 2006.

Martin, Justin. *Rebel Souls: Walt Whitman and America's First Bohemians*. Boston, MA: Da Capo, 2014.

Marx, Karl. *Later Political Writings*. Edited and translated by Terrell Carver. Cambridge: Cambridge University Press, 1996.

Miller, Richard. *Bohemia: The Protoculture Then and Now*. Chicago: Nelson Hall, 1977.

Murger, Henry. *Scenes from the Latin Quarter*. London: Capuchin Classics, 2010.

Norton, Robert E. *Secret Germany: Stefan George and His Circle*. Ithaca, NY: Cornell University Press, 2002.

Parry, Albert. *Garrets and Pretenders: A History of Bohemianism in America*. New York: Covici, Fried, 1933.

Ransome, Arthur. *Bohemia in London*. New York: Dodd, Mead, 1907.

Roe, Sue. *In Montmartre: Picasso, Matisse, and the Birth of Modernist Art*. New York: Penguin, 2014.

Roe, Sue. *In Montparnasse: The Emergence of Surrealism in Paris, from Duchamp to Dalí*. London: Penguin, 2018.

Richardson, Joanna. *The Bohemians:* La Vie de Bohème *in Paris 1830–1914*. South Brunswick, NJ: A. S. Barnes, 1971.

Sanger, Margaret. *The Autobiography of Margaret Sanger*. 1938; Mineola, NY: Dover, 2004.

Sante, Luc. *The Other Paris*. New York: Farrar, Straus and Giroux, 2015.

Segel, Harold B. *Turn-of-the-Century Cabaret: Paris, Barcelona, Berlin, Munich, Vienna, Cracow, Moscow, St. Petersburg, Zurich*. New York: Columbia University Press, 1987.

Seigel, Jerrold. *Bohemian Paris: Culture, Politics, and the Boundaries of Bourgeois Life*. New York: Penguin, 1987.

Sonn, Richard D. *Anarchism and Cultural Politics in Fin de Siècle France*. Lincoln: University of Nebraska Press, 1989.

Stansell, Christine. *American Moderns: Bohemian New York and the Creation of a New Century*. New York: Metropolitan Books, 2000.

Starkie, Enid. *Petrus Borel, the Lycanthrope: His Life and Times*. London: Faber and Faber, 1954.

Strausbaugh, John. *The Village: 400 Years of Beats, Bohemians, Radicals and Rogues: A History of Greenwich Village*. New York: Echo, 2013.

Symons, Arthur. *Colour Studies in Paris*. London: Chapman and Hall, 1918.

Tytell, John. *Naked Angels: The Lives and Literature of the Beat Generation*. New York: McGraw Hill, 1976.

Weisberg, Gabriel P., ed. *Montmartre and the Making of Mass Culture*. New Brunswick, NJ: Rutgers University Press, 2001.

Weston, William J. *Between Bohemia and Suburbia: Boburbia in the USA*. Abington, Oxon: Routledge, 2019.

Williams, John Taylor. *The Shores of Bohemia: A Cape Cod Story, 1910–1960*. New York: Farrar, Straus and Giroux, 2022.

Williams, Orlo. *Vie de Bohème: A Patch of Romantic Paris*. Boston: Richard G. Badger, 1913.

Wilson, Alexandra. *Puccini's "La Boheme."* New York: Oxford University Press, 2021.

Wilson, Elizabeth. *Bohemians: The Glamorous Outcasts*. New Brunswick, NJ: Rutgers University Press, 2000.

Index

Index

ENGLISH LANGUAGE
A Very Short Introduction
Simon Horobin

The English language is spoken by more than a billion people throughout the world. But where did English come from? And how has it evolved into the language used today?

In this *Very Short Introduction* Simon Horobin investigates how we have arrived at the English we know today, and celebrates the way new speakers and new uses mean that it continues to adapt. Engaging with contemporary concerns about correctness, Horobin considers whether such changes are improvements, or evidence of slipping standards. What is the future for the English language? Will Standard English continue to hold sway, or we are witnessing its replacement by newly emerging Englishes?

www.oup.com/vsi